The Civil War Yesterday and Today In Poetry

Donald T. Iannone, Ph.D.

Dedication

To all those with the courage, willingness, compassion, and foresight to prevent a second civil war in America, and to Tyler Somershield, a dear friend whose longstanding passion for the Civil War sparked my initial interest in this critical episode in American history.
You are missed by your family and friends.

Table of Contents

Praise for this Book

"In this compelling book on the Civil War, Don Iannone masterfully uses poetry to merge the power of historical truth with profound emotional depth. His work bridges the gap between what is factual and what is felt, exploring how racism, prejudice, and inequality have persisted since 1865. Don's poetry offers readers both intellectual engagement and emotional resonance, serving as a timely reminder that the possibility of a second civil war looms if conscious action is not taken. A beautifully crafted and thought-provoking work. Truly remarkable!"
~Dr. Lloyd Williams, Ph.D., D. Min.
Chief Academic Officer, Transcontinental University
Tuskegee, Alabama

"The *Civil War Yesterday and Today in Poetry* captures history's echoes with poignant clarity, blending past and present through vivid verse. Each poem is a bridge across centuries, reminding us that the trials of our ancestors are woven into the fabric of today's society. A truly evocative work, this collection compels readers to reflect deeply on America's ongoing journey and the lessons that still resonate."
~Ronnie L. Bryant, CEcD, HLM, FM
Principal, Ronnie L Bryant, LLC
Charlotte, North Carolina

"The Civil War Yesterday and Today in Poetry by Don Iannone is a unique and interesting investigation of America's historical struggle to understand and resolve the internal societal fight for the soul by its people. Using poetry to illustrate the values, beliefs and attitudes of America's people from the Civil War through today, we are informed and understand the feelings and emotions that are the basis for our ongoing deep-seated political, social and economic divisions. I found Don's approach in this book to be a fascinating way to understand our history and think about our future as Americans. Congratulations, this book truly captures the spirit, soul and complexities of America past and present, through poetry. It is a 'Call to Action' for us not to repeat our past, because we refuse to learn from its lessons."
~Gregory L. Brown, Executive Director
PolicyBridge
Cleveland, Ohio

"The Civil War Yesterday and Today in Poetry is a unique and articulate look at American national tensions both recent and decades long passed. Don Iannone has not only assembled a wonderful collection of poetry, but he also provides introductory frameworks for the Civil War and later eras as it relates to poetry and provides biographies of influential Civil War poets."
~Dr. Michael V. Wells, Ph.D.
Associate Professor Emeritus, Urban Studies
Cleveland State University
Cleveland, Ohio

Foreword

In this carefully crafted and well-researched book, Don Iannone uses his poetry as a time machine to carry us back to the years before, during, and after the U.S. Civil War. This time machine transports us into today's world and casts a light into the future. It shows us how power based on privilege, class, race, and wealth more often corrupts than heals a nation and its people.

A civil war is an internal conflict between groups within the same country or state, marked by violent confrontations where warring factions seek control of the government, assert autonomy, or push for significant political or social changes. These conflicts arise from deep divisions—whether ideological, ethnic, religious, or political—that escalate into violence when peaceful resolutions fail. Civil wars often involve groups with distinct visions for governance, power, and rights, driven by feelings of marginalization or oppression. They signal a breakdown of state institutions and destroy social cohesion, leaving lasting political, economic, and humanitarian damage.

The American Civil War remains one of the most defining events in American history, an extremely costly conflict that brought at best temporary justice, which is challenged daily by how Americans live their lives today. This poetic journey traverses 170 years of American history—reaching back to the time before the Civil War, through the conflict itself, into the remainder of the 19th century, and across the 20th and 21st centuries. The poems in this collection go beyond the Civil War's battles to explore the enduring struggles in American society since its founding, reflecting on the deep-seated values and beliefs that have shaped the nation's course.

Through these vivid and often unsettling poems, readers will witness not only the violence and suffering of the Civil War but also the moral and societal battles that have continued to define America. This collection captures the voices of those who fought for freedom, the leaders who wrestled with doubt, and the civilians caught in history's relentless tide. It offers graphic depictions of battlefields and the brutality of slavery, alongside reflections on America's past and present struggles for justice, equality, and democracy. Several of the book's poems serve as fair warning of what the future may hold for our nation and its people.

As you turn the pages, you will walk alongside soldiers, mothers, enslaved people, and leaders, sharing their hopes, fears, and triumphs. This is not just the story of one war, but of a nation's ongoing struggle to realize its ideals. Ultimately, the poems ask us to confront both the darkness and the light within American history and ourselves, offering a raw, emotional look at the challenges that have shaped the United States and continue to do so today. Strap on your seatbelt and prepare for a riveting roller coaster ride through the past into today's severely challenged world.

As America prepares for the next leg of its journey after the 2024 election, we must find a way to bridge our differences and come together as one nation. Let us be guided by our shared and unwavering belief in democracy—a system that, despite its flaws, remains the best path toward freedom, justice, and the common good. Only by uniting our voices can we chart a course for a future that honors our ideals and brings hope to all.

To help navigate unfamiliar terms, names, and events mentioned throughout the book, readers are invited to explore the comprehensive glossary provided at the end of the book.

~C. Ellen Connally, J.D., M.A.
Judge - Retired - Cleveland Municipal Court
Past President, Cuyahoga County Council
Past President of the Cleveland Civil War Roundtable
Vice President of the Cuyahoga County Soldiers and Sailors Monument

Prologue: Road to Our Present Crisis

The U.S. Civil War offers profound lessons on the dangers of extreme polarization within a nation, particularly when political divisions begin to seep into the fabric of everyday life. Prior to the Civil War, America was deeply divided over slavery, economics, and the role of federal versus state power. These divisions were not just confined to political debates in Washington but were reflected in the daily lives of Americans, from the Northern abolitionists to Southern plantation owners. As these ideological rifts deepened, they hardened into entrenched positions, with each side viewing the other as fundamentally incompatible. The South believed its way of life and economic future depended on slavery, while the North increasingly saw slavery as a moral wrong and a threat to the nation's democratic ideals. This stark polarization permeated every aspect of American life, from local communities to religious institutions, ultimately making compromise nearly impossible. The failure to bridge this ideological divide laid the groundwork for civil war.

The Civil War also teaches that once polarization becomes extreme enough, it can transform political disagreements into existential battles. In the years leading up to the war, political institutions became paralyzed as Southern states pushed for the expansion of slavery, while Northern states resisted. The infamous Dred Scott decision in 1857, which ruled that African Americans could never be citizens, further inflamed tensions. When political discourse becomes dominated by such irreconcilable differences, it can leave people feeling that their very existence, rights, and future are at stake. Once a nation reaches this level of political extremism, the usual methods of conflict resolution—compromise, negotiation, and debate—begin to fail. Also, the Civil War shows how polarized politics can spiral into violence when large segments of the population see no other way to secure their vision of the future. It is a stark reminder that unchecked polarization, particularly when amplified by economic, social, and racial divides, can set the stage for civil war, as the rifts between different factions of society become too deep to heal peacefully.

The growing polarization in America that could be seen as leading up to a modern-day civil war became more evident over several decades, with specific dates and events marking deepening divisions. One key moment was the 1960s Civil Rights Movement, which, while advancing equality for African Americans, also exposed deep racial and regional divides that still reverberate today. The violent backlash to desegregation efforts, including the 1965 Selma marches and the Watts riots, highlighted racial tension that simmered beneath the surface of American society.

In the 1970s, the fallout from the Vietnam War and the Watergate scandal further eroded trust in government institutions, fostering an anti-establishment sentiment that continued into later decades. The 1980s saw the rise of Ronald Reagan's presidency and the conservative revolution, which reshaped political discourse, emphasizing free markets, small government, and strong nationalism. Reagan's policies led to growing economic disparities between the rich and poor, setting the stage for the resentment that would later fuel political divides.

By the time Bill Clinton was elected in 1992, the ideological battle lines had begun to harden between a more progressive, multicultural vision of America and a conservative base resistant to social change. This became particularly evident with events like the 1994 Contract with America, led by Newt Gingrich, which initiated a period of intense partisanship in Congress. The impeachment of Clinton in 1998 underscored how deeply divided the nation had become, with political fights turning increasingly personal and vitriolic.

In the 2000s, the attacks of September 11, 2001, initially brought a sense of national unity, but the ensuing War on Terror, particularly the invasion of Iraq in 2003, exposed new fault lines. Public opinion became sharply divided over issues of national security, foreign policy, and the role of government surveillance, leading to protests and a growing anti-war movement. At the same time, the economic collapse in 2008 during the Great Recession worsened economic inequality, with middle-class and working-class Americans feeling left behind by globalization and the financial industry's recovery, further polarizing rich and poor.

The election of Barack Obama in 2008 marked another pivotal moment in American polarization. While historic as the first Black president, Obama's presidency deepened racial and political divisions, particularly as conservative backlash grew. The rise of the Tea Party movement in 2009 reflected dissatisfaction with Obama's policies on health care, government spending, and immigration, highlighting growing resentment among more conservative and rural voters who felt alienated from the Democratic Party's vision of America.

The Christian right has also played a critical role in shaping modern American politics, particularly since the 1980s. Spearheaded by leaders like Jerry Falwell and Pat Robertson, the Christian right aligned itself with the Republican Party, championing issues like abortion, traditional family values, and opposition to same-sex marriage. By framing these issues as moral imperatives, they mobilized a significant portion of the electorate, often amplifying the culture wars that have divided the country. In recent years, the

Christian right has become a dominant force in shaping the GOP's stance on issues like religious freedom, the role of government in regulating personal behavior, and the fight against perceived liberal cultural overreach. This movement has helped cement a powerful ideological divide in American politics, particularly around issues of faith, family, morality, and social justice.

These tensions culminated in the election of Donald Trump in 2016, a moment that crystallized the deepening divides within the country. Trump's populist and nationalist rhetoric, focusing on issues like immigration, trade, and law and order, resonated with disenfranchised voters, particularly in rural and industrial regions that had seen economic decline. The 2017 Charlottesville rally, where white nationalists clashed with counter-protesters, vividly illustrated how race and identity had become central to the political conflict. At the same time, the growing power of movements like Black Lives Matter emphasized the widening gap between those calling for social justice and those resisting demographic and cultural shifts.

The 2020 COVID-19 pandemic exacerbated these divides, with debates over government intervention, public health measures, and economic recovery fueling intense polarization. Disagreements over mask mandates, vaccine requirements, and the role of science versus individual liberty revealed a lack of national consensus on how to manage a crisis. The January 6, 2021, insurrection at the U.S. Capitol marked one of the most significant signs of this polarization manifesting in violence, as disputes over the legitimacy of the 2020 election boiled over.

Donald Trump's victory over Kamala Harris in the 2024 presidential election underscores the deepening ideological divides within the United States. Harris's campaign emphasized progressive ideals, including climate action, social justice, and the protection of voting rights. In a remarkably short period of time, Kamala Harris swiftly organized and launched a presidential campaign, demonstrating her skill and determination on the national stage. Though she didn't secure the victory, she fought with conviction and left a lasting impact on the race.

In contrast, Trump's platform centered on nationalism, populism, economic growth, and resistance to perceived federal overreach and progressive cultural values. The Republicans ran a highly effective campaign, marked by sharp messaging, strategic voter outreach, and a keen understanding of the political landscape.

Several key factors contributed to Trump's success:

1. **Economic Concerns**: Trump's focus on economic issues, particularly tax cuts, deregulation, inflation, and job creation, resonated with voters concerned about their financial well-being. His promises to revitalize the economy and reduce inflation appealed to many, especially in rural areas and swing states.

2. **Immigration Policies**: Trump's strong stance on immigration,

including pledges to secure the borders and implement strict immigration controls, attracted voters prioritizing national security and sovereignty.

3. **Cultural Issues**: Trump effectively tapped into cultural and social issues, positioning himself as a defender of traditional values against progressive changes. This approach garnered support from voters feeling alienated by rapid cultural shifts.

4. **Campaign Strategy**: Despite internal disagreements, Trump's unconventional campaign methods, including leveraging social media and alternative media platforms, allowed him to connect directly with voters and bypass traditional media scrutiny.

The election results reflect a nation deeply divided along ideological lines, with each side viewing the other as an existential threat to the country's future. This polarization has led to an environment where compromise is increasingly elusive, and political conflict appears more likely with each passing election.

I chose poetry as a vehicle to communicate about the US Civil War and the potential for another civil war in America because it allows for a deeper emotional connection, offers a reflective space for confronting hard truths, and provides a powerful means to distill complex issues into resonant, thought-provoking imagery. Poetry transcends factual recounting, capturing the human spirit, the raw pain of division, and the urgency of the lessons history must teach us.

Next Up: Chapter 1: Key Book Takeaways: The next chapter identifies in summary form the main points made in "The Civil War Yesterday and Today in Poetry."

Chapter 1: Key Book Takeaways

1. The American journey, from the mid-1800s through the present, is captured in the lines of poetry that navigate the nation's core struggles—inequality, race, human suffering, political power, extreme wealth and poverty, and economic transformation. In these poems by Don Iannone, the battle for the soul of America is a recurring theme, with deep divisions rooted in the pre-Civil War era, intensifying through the war itself, and reshaping across Reconstruction, industrialization, civil rights movements, and the present-day landscape of political polarization.

2. The book's examination of Civil War poetry, from its historical roots to modern interpretations, reveals a deep engagement with themes of loss, sacrifice, and ideological division. Civil War poetry from the 19th century reflected the personal and collective struggles of soldiers, officers, medics, and chaplains, with poets like Walt Whitman and Henry Timrod capturing the emotional toll of the war. Whitman, for instance, expressed themes of mourning and leadership in "O Captain! My Captain!" while Timrod's work like "Ethnogenesis" celebrated the Confederate cause. Both Northern and Southern poets used their art to explore their respective political positions—Northern poets focusing on abolition and preserving the Union, and Southern poets romanticizing the fight for independence and the values of the agrarian South. Poetry became an important means of reflecting on the human cost of war and the deep ideological divides between North and South.

In recent years, contemporary poets have returned to the Civil War as a subject to explore the ways in which those divisions still shape modern America. The 2013 Lines in Long Array project, for example, commissioned poets such as Yusef Komunyakaa and Nikki Giovanni to reflect on the Civil War's legacy in today's political and racial landscape. These modern poets often link the unresolved tensions of the Civil War, especially concerning race, to present-day issues like systemic racism and political extremism. The rediscovery of African American Civil War poetry from the Anglo-African and National Anti-Slavery Standard newspapers, which features 19th century writers like Fanny M. Jackson and William Slade, has further enriched our understanding of how marginalized voices contributed to wartime discourse. These poems, long forgotten, highlight the complexities of African American involvement in the Civil War and their hopes for freedom and equality. The connection between past and present becomes evident through these modern poetic works, as writers use the Civil War to discuss contemporary political divisions and the threat of a modern-day civil conflict. In this context, poetry serves as both a historical record and a tool for contemporary reflection, helping readers understand the ongoing impact of the Civil War and its unresolved legacies in America.

3.   Pre-Civil War America is the backdrop for understanding the nation's fundamental conflicts. Poems in this section evoke the institution of slavery and its grip on the South's agrarian economy, a force that not only fueled growth but created an irreconcilable divide. Political compromises like the Missouri Compromise and the Compromise of 1850 are painted in verses showing a fragile union strained by moral contradictions. Abolitionist voices rise in the poems, echoing the North's industrial expansion and calling for a new vision of America—one that sees human beings as free, equal, and not property. The inevitable eruption of the Civil War is captured through stirring poems about John Brown's raid and the Dred Scott decision, which exposed the gulf between these opposing visions.

4.   Civil War America is brought to life in raw and poignant poetry about the bloodiest conflict in U.S. history. The poems chronicle a war of attrition, sacrifice, and conviction. Verses about Lincoln's leadership and generals like Grant and Lee illustrate the war's physical and ideological battles. Poems inspired by the Emancipation Proclamation give voice to the war's moral reframing, focusing not only on union but on the fight for human freedom. The Battle of Gettysburg and other key turning points appear in solemn and reflective lines, but the real impact, woven through the poems, is the reshaping of American society. Through the voices of women, enslaved people, and soldiers, these poems remind us that the war's conclusion abolished slavery but left deep wounds—racial, regional, and emotional—that linger.

5.   Post-Civil War America enters a time of transformation and missed opportunities. The Reconstruction poems resonate with the hope of rebuilding the South and the nation's effort to redefine citizenship. The passage of the 13th, 14th, and 15th Amendments is a beacon of progress in the verses, but alongside it rises the darker poetry of Jim Crow, white supremacy, and the disenfranchisement of Black

Americans. Sharecropping, tenant farming, and poverty are recurring images in this section's poems, juxtaposed with the North's embrace of industrial capitalism. The expansion of railroads and the birth of modern cities are captured through poetic snapshots, with verses acknowledging labor struggles, political corruption, and growing inequality.

6. The 20th Century is marked by America's rise as a global superpower, with poems that explore the contradictions between this ascent and continued domestic strife. The Progressive Era poems shed light on labor reforms, women's suffrage, and antitrust battles. Yet, the poems also reflect the wars of the century—World War I, World War II—and how these conflicts expanded roles for African Americans, women, and immigrants, while failing to erase discrimination. Poetry of the Great Depression and the New Deal traces the fragility of the American economy, and later poems reflect the civil rights movements of the 1960s, with victories and setbacks chronicled in verse. From Brown v. Board of Education to the conservative backlash of the late 20th century, the poems speak to a country grappling with its values. Poems on economic globalization and immigration address the reshaping of industries, while those on deindustrialization and labor struggles evoke feelings of instability.

7. 21st-Century America finds itself echoing the unresolved struggles of the past, with poetry reflecting the nation's engagement with global and domestic challenges. The post-9/11 world is portrayed in lines that discuss the War on Terrorism, prolonged wars in the Middle East, and the Great Recession of 2008, which widened the economic divide. Political polarization becomes a central theme in the poems, from the election of Barack Obama to the rise of Trumpism. Movements like #MeToo and Black Lives Matter find expression in poetry that challenges sexism, systemic racism, and inequality, continuing the legacy of civil rights. The COVID-19 pandemic is also chronicled in verses that expose weaknesses in America's health, social, and economic systems, offering reflections on how the country's future remains deeply tied to the past's unresolved questions: What does equality mean? Who can fully participate in the American dream? And how can a divided nation move forward?

Next Up: Chapter 2 provides a critical review of Civil War poetry, both past and present, with an emphasis on the importance and impact of poetry in sparking thoughts and feelings about the Civil War and its aftermath.

Chapter 2: Review of Civil War Poetry

Power of Poetry in the Civil War: An Historical and Literary Critique

The American Civil War was one of the most defining and devastating moments in U.S. history, with poetry playing a significant role in reflecting, shaping, and interpreting the cultural and emotional landscape of the time. Through poems, people expressed their hopes, griefs, loyalties, and, most of all, the tensions that tore the nation apart. Poetry was an essential vehicle for both the Union and the Confederacy, providing a means to communicate the human experience of the war and offer ideological justifications or emotional appeals.

The Role of Poetry in the Civil War

During the Civil War, poetry served as a key medium for personal expression and public discourse. Newspapers, magazines, and broadsides printed poems that ranged from rallying cries for soldiers to heart-wrenching depictions of the war's toll on families and communities. Poetry offered solace, motivation, and reflection. In a pre-television era, when mass communication was limited to print media, poetry was a form of instant commentary on the war, allowing people to process events as they unfolded.

For many, poetry functioned as a moral compass, navigating the complex issues of loyalty, honor, sacrifice, and the struggle for freedom. It was also a cultural tool to reflect the ideological divides between North and South, with each side offering distinct perspectives on liberty, state rights, and union.

Prominent Poets and Poems

Although not all poets of the Civil War era were soldiers, many writers used their art to engage with the war's profound themes of division, death, and national identity. Below are some of the most important poets and their contributions during the war:

Walt Whitman

Walt Whitman, perhaps the most famous Civil War poet, brought a compassionate humanism to his poetry. Whitman served as a nurse during the war, tending to wounded soldiers, and his experiences deeply influenced his writing. His poems, such as "O Captain! My Captain!" and "When Lilacs Last in the Dooryard Bloom'd," mourned the assassination of President

Abraham Lincoln and explored themes of leadership, loss, and mourning. His poem "Beat! Beat! Drums!" captures the sense of urgency and mobilization at the beginning of the war.

Whitman's poetry stands out for its blend of realism and lyricism. He brought a democratic vision to his work, emphasizing the common soldier, the human body, and the deep connection between the personal and the national. His poems remain essential for understanding how the war touched everyday lives.

Emily Dickinson

Though Emily Dickinson did not engage directly with the politics of the Civil War, her poetry captures the era's intense emotions, often exploring themes of death, loss, and mortality. Her poem "My Portion is Defeat — today" conveys a profound sense of grief that resonates with the nation's collective mourning. Dickinson's ability to capture the complexity of sorrow in concise, evocative lines mirrored the emotional turmoil of the war years.

Henry Timrod

Known as the "Laureate of the Confederacy," Henry Timrod's poetry reflected the Southern cause with patriotic zeal. His poem "Ethnogenesis," written at the birth of the Confederacy, captures the South's aspirations for independence and pride in their new nation. Timrod's poetry was widely read and used to rally Confederate soldiers, but it also expressed the sorrow of the South's eventual defeat. His poem "The Cotton Boll" emphasized the economic importance of cotton and how the war was tied to the South's agrarian life, bringing in nature and nostalgia as symbols of Southern identity.

John Greenleaf Whittier

A fervent abolitionist, Whittier's poetry was often polemical, using moral argument to critique slavery and the war. His work, such as "The Slave's Appeal," pushed the anti-slavery agenda of the Union and reflected the Northern belief in the righteousness of the abolitionist cause. Unlike some poets, Whittier's work was grounded in a sense of moral duty and social justice, making his poetry part of the larger abolitionist movement in the North.

Herman Melville

Though better known for Moby-Dick, Herman Melville also wrote powerful poetry about the Civil War. His collection Battle-Pieces and Aspects of the War (1866) offers a sobering reflection on the costs of the conflict, grappling with the violence and suffering it caused. His poem "Shiloh" is a somber meditation on the dead after a battle, a far cry from the celebratory patriotism of other war poets. Melville's work reminds us of the profound human costs of war.

The Geography of Poetry: North vs. South

Civil War poetry thrived both in the North and the South, though the subject matter and tone often varied between the two regions. In the North, poetry was largely focused on the themes of union, abolition, and justice. Abolitionist poets like Whittier and the moral authority of Lincoln were central to the Northern poetic imagination. Northern poets also dealt with the personal grief of loss, as in Whitman's "Vigil Strange I Kept on the Field One Night," where the speaker mourns a fallen comrade.

In contrast, Southern poetry often reflected themes of honor, chivalry, and nostalgia for an agrarian past. Poets like Henry Timrod and Sidney Lanier (who wrote post-war) idealized the Southern way of life, focusing on the nobility of the Confederate cause, even as the South faced defeat. The South's use of poetry to justify secession and to express sorrow at its losses gave it a distinct emotional flavor. Southern poetry also dealt with the trauma of a destroyed society, encapsulating the regional pride that persisted even after the war's conclusion.

It is difficult to say which side produced more poetry; however, poetry likely held equal significance across both regions as a tool for morale and identity. Southern poets like Timrod were well-known in the South, while Northern poets like Whitman and Whittier were more prominent in Union states.

Subject Matter of Civil War Poetry

Civil War poetry often dealt with themes of death, honor, sacrifice, and the broader struggle between good and evil. For the North, poetry was a platform to address slavery, emancipation, and the preservation of the Union. Many poems captured the harrowing reality of the battlefield, the grief of families, and the psychological trauma that soldiers experienced.

In the South, poetry was more likely to romanticize the cause of the Confederacy, focusing on the valor of soldiers and the nobility of Southern culture. There was also a significant amount of elegiac poetry in both the North and South, as poets sought to memorialize the countless dead on both sides.

One common theme across Civil War poetry was the idea of a nation fractured, with poets grappling with what the war meant for the future of the United States. Poems asked existential questions about the nature of freedom, loyalty, and human suffering.

Lessons from Civil War Poetry

Today, Civil War poetry offers valuable insights into the mindset of the people who lived through the conflict. It provides us with intimate accounts of the emotional and psychological toll the war took on the nation, and through its verses, we can better understand the ideological battles fought both on and off the battlefield.

From a literary perspective, Civil War poetry demonstrates how art can serve as a powerful reflection of social and political climates. It also reminds us that poetry is not merely a passive reflection of events, but an active participant in the shaping of public sentiment. Whether through Whitman's empathetic humanism, Timrod's Southern idealism, or Melville's philosophical meditations, we can see how poets responded to the war's enormity.

More broadly, Civil War poetry provides us with timeless lessons about the human costs of conflict, the complexities of national identity, and the power of words to both heal and divide. These poems continue to resonate in modern times, offering reminders of the delicate nature of union, the persistence of ideological conflict, and the enduring need for empathy and reflection in times of division.

In conclusion, Civil War poetry is more than a historical artifact—it is a rich, vibrant body of work that continues to speak to contemporary readers about war, loss, and the human condition. As we reflect on these poems today, they offer a poignant reminder of the fragility of peace and the enduring strength of the human spirit in the face of national turmoil.

Poetry Written by Soldiers, Officers, Medics, and Chaplains in the American Civil War

The American Civil War was not only a clash of armies and ideologies but also a deeply personal conflict for those directly involved. Soldiers, officers, medics, and chaplains—all individuals directly touched by the realities of war—contributed their voices to the broader literary canon through poetry. Their poems offer invaluable insights into the experiences, emotions, and reflections of those who lived through one of the bloodiest conflicts in American history. These poems were often written in moments of solitude, either during the lull of battle, in hospitals, or in the aftermath of profound loss, providing raw and intimate perspectives on war.

This chapter explores the significance of poetry written by those who were directly part of the Civil War, analyzing the themes, motivations, and lasting impact of their work. We look at the poetry of soldiers, officers, medics, and chaplains, examining how they used poetry to process the horrors of war, express personal and collective grief, and articulate their hopes and fears.

The Role of Poetry for Soldiers and Officers

Soldiers on both sides of the Civil War, from common foot soldiers to high-ranking officers, used poetry to grapple with the overwhelming emotions they experienced on and off the battlefield. These poems often reflected the stark realities of war—fear, loneliness, and the ever-present specter of death. They also served as letters home, memorials for fallen comrades, and reflections on the larger cause for which they fought.

Poetry as Emotional Catharsis

For many soldiers, poetry was a means of emotional release. In an era when expressing vulnerability was often seen as a weakness, especially in a military context, poetry provided a way to convey the deepest of fears and sorrows without compromising a soldier's sense of duty or masculinity. These poems were often intensely personal, revealing the inner lives of men who otherwise appeared stoic or hardened by battle.

Example: "The Dying Soldier" by an unknown Confederate soldier

In one stirring example, a Confederate soldier penned a poem titled "The Dying Soldier," which captures the anguish and resignation of a soldier confronting his own death on the battlefield. The poem describes the physical pain of his wounds and the deep sorrow of dying far from home, offering a glimpse into the intimate and human side of the soldier's experience. The poem ends with the soldier imagining his family mourning his death, a reminder of the personal sacrifices made by those who fought.

Poetry as Propaganda and Ideological Justification

Military officers used poetry to articulate their understanding of the broader cause. Whether fighting for the Union or the Confederacy, officers often took a more philosophical or reflective approach to war poetry, considering the moral, political, and ideological implications of the conflict. These poems were not just personal musings but often served as justifications for the war and calls to arms for others.

Union officers, for example, frequently invoked the fight for freedom and the preservation of the Union. Their poetry reflected the belief that the war was a necessary evil to achieve a higher moral good—namely, the abolition of slavery and the defense of democracy. Confederate officers, by contrast, framed their poetry around concepts of honor, state rights, and the defense of Southern culture.

Example: "Lines Written on the Eve of Battle" by Colonel William Haines Lytle

Colonel William Haines Lytle, a Union officer who was also a poet before the war, wrote "Lines Written on the Eve of Battle" shortly before he was killed at the Battle of Chickamauga in 1863. The poem is a moving reflection on duty, sacrifice, and the inevitable approach of death. Lytle, knowing that he might die in battle, writes with both resignation and determination, capturing the emotional complexity faced by officers who bore the responsibility of leading men into combat.

Poems as Letters to Loved Ones

Many soldiers wrote poetry as a form of communication with their loved ones back home. These poems often took the place of letters, serving as poetic snapshots of life at the front. In these works, soldiers expressed longing for home, anxiety about their futures, and the hope that their sacrifices would be understood and appreciated by their families. Some of these poems are heartbreaking in their vulnerability, revealing the deep sense of isolation felt by soldiers far from their loved ones.

Poetry Written by Medics and Chaplains

While soldiers and officers were engaged directly in combat, medics and chaplains witnessed the war from a different perspective. Their poetry often reflects the trauma they experienced in witnessing the physical and spiritual toll of the war. Medics were responsible for tending to the wounded, often under grim and desperate conditions, while chaplains sought to provide spiritual comfort to soldiers facing death or moral despair. Both roles provided a unique vantage point for understanding the war's impact on the human body and soul.

Medics' Poetry: The Brutality of War's Physical Toll

Medics, often unheralded in historical accounts of the Civil War, dealt with the brutal realities of battlefield injuries, amputations, and disease. Their poetry is marked by a visceral depiction of suffering and the often futile attempts to save lives. They witnessed the full extent of human pain, and their poetry reflects a deep sense of helplessness in the face of overwhelming carnage.

Example: "Surgeon's Dream" by an Unknown Union Medic

In the poem "Surgeon's Dream," written by an unknown Union medic, the poet describes the seemingly endless flow of wounded men arriving at the makeshift hospitals after a battle. The poet recounts the frantic pace of amputation surgeries, the cries of the injured, and the stench of blood, highlighting the horrific conditions faced by medics. The poem reflects not only the physical toll on the soldiers but also the emotional exhaustion of the medics themselves.

Chaplains' Poetry: Spiritual Reflection and Mourning

Chaplains played a critical role in providing spiritual care to soldiers, often offering prayers and comfort to the dying. Their poetry frequently wrestles with questions of faith and mortality, offering both comfort and reflection on the religious implications of the war. Chaplains were often asked to reconcile the violence of war with the Christian ideals of love, forgiveness, and peace, and their poetry reflects this tension.

Example: Poems by Father Abram Joseph Ryan

Father Abram Joseph Ryan, known as the "Poet-Priest of the South," was a Confederate chaplain whose poetry expressed a deep sense of Southern loss and mourning. His poem "The Conquered Banner," written after the Confederacy's defeat, became a beloved elegy for the fallen Southern cause. Ryan's poetry is marked by religious imagery, invoking God's will and the hope of redemption even in defeat. His work illustrates how chaplains used poetry to offer spiritual solace to soldiers who had experienced profound trauma and loss.

Themes and Subject Matter in Civil War Poetry by Those Involved

The poetry written by soldiers, officers, medics, and chaplains often shared common themes, but the subject matter also varied depending on their individual experiences of the war. Some of the most prominent themes include:

Death and Mortality

The omnipresence of death is perhaps the most common theme in Civil War poetry written by those directly involved in the conflict. Soldiers and officers faced death in battle, medics dealt with it daily in hospitals, and chaplains ministered to those at the brink of it. The poetry grapples with the inevitability of death and the emotional toll it took on individuals, families, and communities.

Honor and Duty

For many soldiers and officers, poetry became a way to reaffirm their commitment to the cause, whether for the Union or the Confederacy. They used poetry to express their sense of honor, duty, and loyalty to their comrades, and to reflect on the nobility (or futility) of their sacrifice.

Grief and Loss

The overwhelming grief of losing comrades, friends, and family members in the war is another central theme. Poetry offered a way to memorialize those who had died, creating lasting tributes that preserved the memory of the fallen. This sense of collective mourning is particularly poignant in the work of chaplains, whose poems often dealt with the moral and spiritual consequences of so much loss.

Homesickness and Longing

For many soldiers, particularly those who spent years away from their families, poetry was a means to express their longing for home and their desire to return to the lives they had left behind. These poems are filled with nostalgia for domestic life and hope for eventual reunion with loved ones.

The Brutality of War

Medics and some soldiers used poetry to document the sheer brutality of the war, offering unflinching accounts of bloodshed, suffering, and the inhuman conditions of battlefields and hospitals. These poems often serve as testimonies to the horrors of war, preserving the physical and emotional scars inflicted on those who lived through it.

The Blue and the Gray: A Poem by Francis Miles Finch (1867)

"By the flow of the inland river, Whence the fleets of iron have fled, Where the blades of the grave-grass quiver, Asleep are the ranks of the dead: Under the sod and the dew, Waiting the judgment-day; Under the one, the Blue; Under the other, the Gray.

These in the robings of glory, Those in the gloom of defeat, All with the battle-blood gory, In the dusk of eternity meet: Under the sod and the dew, Waiting the judgment-day; Under the laurel, the Blue; Under the willow, the Gray.

From the silence of sorrowful hours The desolate mourners go, Lovingly laden with flowers Alike for the friend and the foe: Under the sod and the dew, Waiting the judgment-day; Under the roses, the Blue; Under the lilies, the Gray.

So with an equal splendor, The morning sun-rays fall, With a touch impartially tender, On the blossoms blooming for all: Under the sod and the dew, Waiting the judgment-day; Broidered with gold, the Blue; Mellowed with gold, the Gray.

So, when the summer calleth, On forest and field of grain, With an equal murmur falleth The cooling drip of the rain: Under the sod and the dew, Waiting the judgment-day; Wet with the rain, the Blue; Wet with the rain, the Gray.

Sadly, but not with upbraiding, The generous deed was done, In the storm of the years that are fading No braver battle was won: Under the sod and the dew, Waiting the judgment-day; Under the blossoms, the Blue; Under the garlands, the Gray.

No more shall the war-cry sever, Or the winding rivers be red; They banish our anger forever When they laurel the graves of our dead! Under the sod and the dew, Waiting the judgment-day; Love and tears for the Blue; Tears and love for the Gray."

"The Blue and the Gray" by Francis Miles Finch reflects on the shared sacrifices of Union (Blue) and Confederate (Gray) soldiers during the Civil War. Inspired by an 1866 event where women in Columbus, Mississippi, decorated the graves of both Union and Confederate soldiers, the poem emphasizes reconciliation and unity. It portrays the fallen from both sides as equally honorable, urging the nation to heal by honoring all who perished, regardless of their allegiance.

What We Can Learn from Civil War Poetry Today

Civil War poetry written by those directly involved in the conflict provides an insightful window into the personal and collective experiences of war. It offers invaluable historical testimony, capturing the thoughts, emotions, and reflections of those who witnessed the conflict firsthand. These poems remind us of the complexity of human experience in wartime—how individuals grapple with fear, courage, grief, and the struggle to make sense of violence on such a massive scale.

Furthermore, these poems offer timeless insights into the nature of war itself. They speak to the human cost of conflict, the deep emotional scars left behind, and the difficulty of reconciling ideals with the harsh realities of combat. The poetry of soldiers, officers, medics, and chaplains provides a powerful counterpoint to

In recent years, several poets have revisited the Civil War, exploring its implications for modern America and the potential threat of another civil conflict. This revival of interest often reflects a growing concern about contemporary political polarization, the persistence of racial divides, and the ongoing debates around the legacy of the Civil War. Contemporary poets use the Civil War not just as a historical moment but as a lens through which they examine modern struggles, including issues of race, democracy, and national identity.

One recent project mentioned earlier, Lines in Long Array, published by the Smithsonian, commissioned twelve poets to reflect on the Civil War in the context of today's political and cultural environment. The poets grapple with the echoes of history, highlighting how many of the tensions that divided the country in the 1860s persist. Contributors like Yusef Komunyakaa and Nikki Giovanni, for instance, delve into themes of race, memory, and the cost of conflict, connecting the historical Civil War to contemporary issues like racial inequality and the ongoing struggles for civil rights.

The legacy of the Civil War remains fertile ground for poetry, especially as racial injustice and political fragmentation continue to dominate American discourse. Poets like Steve Scafidi have written about figures such as Abraham Lincoln and John Brown, using them as symbols to reflect on the unresolved nature of America's racial and ideological conflicts. Scafidi, for instance, explores the duality of John Brown—depicting him as both a freedom fighter and a figure of violence, paralleling modern debates over the use of force in the pursuit of justice .

Another important recovery of Civil War poetry is from 19th century African American publications like the Anglo-African and the National Anti-Slavery Standard. These newspapers published poems from African American writers who used poetry to engage in public debates about emancipation and African American enlistment in the Union Army. The recovery of these poems, many of which had been forgotten for over a century, offers valuable insights into the African American experience during the war and highlights the transatlantic dimensions of the conflict. These poems provide perspectives on love, loss, hope, and the political stakes of the war, all of which resonate with contemporary readers who see parallels in today's struggles over racial equality .

In sum, modern poets have found in the Civil War a powerful metaphor for the divisions that still threaten America today. The resurgence of Civil War poetry reflects an ongoing process of reckoning with the war's legacy, reminding readers of the unresolved issues of race, identity, and national unity that continue to shape the country. By engaging with the past, poets help illuminate the potential dangers of repeating history, using the war as a cautionary tale for a nation still grappling with the possibility of a new civil conflict. The resurgence of poetry reflecting on the American Civil War and its implications for today's political and social environment is a powerful artistic response to the growing concerns of modern political polarization, racial divisions, and threats to democracy. Contemporary poets use the Civil War as a lens to analyze today's cultural landscape, drawing connections between the historical conflict and the unresolved tensions that still pervade American society. This essay explores the contemporary poetry landscape that revisits the Civil War, focusing on its themes, historical context, and how it relates to fears of a modern-day civil conflict.

The Threat of a Modern-Day Civil War

Political Polarization and Echoes of the Past

Modern poets have increasingly drawn parallels between the Civil War era and the present-day polarization of American society. "The Civil War Yesterday and Today in Poetry" can be appropriately understood in this light. As the country grapples with stark divisions along political, racial, and ideological lines, poets are using the Civil War as a framework to explore the potential consequences of these divides. Writers like Nikki Giovanni warn of the dangers of allowing history to repeat itself, highlighting how unresolved issues from the 19th century continue to fuel contemporary conflicts.

Civil War Poetry as Social Critique

Many contemporary poets view their work as a social critique, using the Civil War as a powerful lens through which they warn of the fragility of democracy and the unresolved tensions that still haunt America. Poets like Natasha Trethewey and Claudia Rankine reflect on the past to show how the nation's failure to fully confront the legacy of slavery and racial violence has left it vulnerable to new and deepening divisions. Trethewey's poetry often navigates the complexities of historical memory and the lingering scars of slavery, particularly in works like Native Guard, which brings the hidden stories of African American soldiers to light. Similarly, Rankine, in her widely acclaimed Citizen, dissects the subtle and overt racial injustices that permeate modern society, drawing direct lines from the Civil War's legacy to the struggles for racial justice today. These poets urge readers to recognize that America's historical wounds have not healed but have instead festered, contributing to the nation's ongoing battles over identity, equality, and justice.

The Role of Memory in Modern Civil Conflict

One of the most profound ways in which Civil War poetry resonates today is through its exploration of memory—how a nation remembers its past and how those memories shape its present. Poets like Dave Smith reflect on the idea that the Civil War is not just a historical event but a living memory that continues to influence American identity and politics. As Smith notes, "the past isn't dead. It isn't even past," a sentiment that speaks to how the unresolved tensions of the Civil War era continue to inform modern political and cultural divides .

Lessons from Contemporary Civil War Poetry

The resurgence of poetry about the Civil War offers critical lessons for today's America. First, it underscores the importance of confronting history honestly and directly. Many contemporary poets argue that the failure to fully address the legacy of slavery and the Civil War has allowed racial and political divisions to fester, making the possibility of renewed conflict more likely. This poetry serves as a call to action, urging Americans to learn from the past rather than repeat its mistakes.

Second, these poems remind readers of the human cost of division. Whether reflecting on the personal grief of leaders like Lincoln or the experiences of enslaved people fighting for freedom, Civil War poetry provides a stark reminder that ideological conflicts often come at a profound human cost. In an era of increasing polarization, these poems encourage empathy and understanding as a means of bridging divides.

Lastly, contemporary Civil War poetry highlights the role of art and literature in shaping public discourse. By revisiting the Civil War through a modern lens, poets contribute to the ongoing debate about America's identity, its values, and its future. In doing so, they offer a powerful reminder of the ways in which literature can influence national consciousness and help societies reckon with their past.

Political Extremism and Deep Cleavages: Modern Poetry's Reflection on the American Ideological Divide

In today's politically polarized landscape, poets have increasingly turned their attention to the ideological cleavages that divide American society. The rise of political extremism, growing cultural and social divides, and debates over core beliefs and values have provided fertile ground for poets to explore the tensions threatening national unity. Through their work, modern poets express the anxieties of a nation grappling with fractured identities and shifting political landscapes. They examine the dangers of extremism, the deep emotional and cultural divisions in society, and the consequences of ideological rigidities.

The Role of Poetry in Addressing Political Extremism

Poetry has long been a vehicle for addressing societal and political unrest, and in the current climate, it remains a vital medium through which modern writers engage with these deep-seated tensions. As political extremism has become more prominent, poets have used their work to reflect on the fear, anger, and division that characterize American life.

As mentioned earlier, poet Claudia Rankine, in her acclaimed work Citizen: An American Lyric, addresses the intersection of race, identity, and systemic inequality in contemporary America. Through prose poems and essays, Rankine examines the subtle and overt forms of racism embedded in society, presenting these as part of the larger ideological struggles that deepen the divisions between different racial and cultural groups in the U.S. Her work directly engages with political extremism by addressing the consequences of hate speech, racial violence, and exclusionary ideologies that marginalize minority communities .

Similarly, Terrance Hayes, in his collection American Sonnets for My Past and Future Assassin, uses the sonnet form to explore political and cultural tensions in America, especially following the 2016 presidential election. Hayes reflects on the rise of white supremacy, systemic racism, and authoritarianism, depicting the speaker's struggle to navigate a country increasingly defined by polarization and extremism. The poem series captures the sense of urgency and crisis, as Hayes grapples with what it means to live in a society that is fracturing along ideological and racial lines .

Poetry Reflecting Deep Cleavages in American Society

In addition to political extremism, many modern poets explore the deep cultural and ideological divides that characterize contemporary American society. These divides are often rooted in divergent beliefs about religion, race, immigration, gender, and the nature of democracy itself. Poetry serves as a means of reflecting on these tensions, offering both personal and collective perspectives on how Americans navigate their divided identities.

Amanda Gorman, whose poetry gained widespread attention following her performance at President Biden's inauguration, often addresses themes of national unity in the face of division. In her inaugural poem, The Hill We Climb, Gorman speaks directly to the ideological cleavages in America, acknowledging the deep wounds left by political extremism, systemic inequality, and violence. Yet, Gorman's work also emphasizes hope and the possibility of healing, suggesting that poetry can serve as a bridge between opposing sides of the ideological spectrum .

Likewise, Tracy K. Smith, former U.S. Poet Laureate, addresses the ideological divides that permeate American life in her collection Wade in the Water. In poems that deal with slavery, racial inequality, and American identity, Smith reflects on the long history of division in the United States, tracing how these historical injustices continue to influence modern debates over race, identity, and power. Her poetry speaks to the enduring legacy of division and the difficulties of reconciliation in a deeply divided society.

The Intersection of Beliefs, Values, and Extremism in Modern Poetry

A key element of modern poetry on American division is the examination of how differing beliefs and values contribute to societal fractures. Poets like Ocean Vuong delve into the personal impacts of these ideological divides, exploring how they manifest within families and communities. Vuong's work often touches on themes of identity, immigration, and the immigrant experience in America, offering poignant reflections on the sense of alienation and belonging in a country that struggles with inclusion and acceptance of the "other." His poetry reflects the emotional toll of being caught between different cultures and ideologies, often with deeply personal resonance.

Poets such as Layli Long Soldier engage with the historical injustices faced by Indigenous people and the ideological erasure of their histories. Her collection Whereas responds to the formal apology issued by the U.S. government to Native peoples, and through this work, Long Soldier examines the gulf between rhetoric and reality. Her poetry interrogates the values that underpin American identity and calls attention to the ideological and cultural violence inflicted on Indigenous communities.

Poetry as a Reflection of Contemporary Fears and Hopes

While many poets focus on the dangers of ideological extremism and the deep divisions within American society, others offer visions of hope and healing. Joy Harjo, a past U.S. Poet Laureate and the first Native American to hold the position, frequently writes about the possibility of unity through shared cultural memory and healing. In her work, Harjo emphasizes the need for storytelling and understanding as antidotes to division, advocating for a collective reimagining of what it means to be American in the face of historical and contemporary injustices.

Poetry that addresses the deep cleavages in American society often carries a dual purpose: it bears witness to the pain of division while also imagining the possibility of repair. Through their work, poets are not only chronicling the tensions that define modern America but are also contributing to the national conversation about how to bridge these divides and create a more inclusive society.

Modern Poets Expressing Themselves as Conservatives and Liberals: Exploring Political Divides in Contemporary American Poetry

In today's politically charged climate, poetry remains a vibrant medium for reflecting on ideological divides, with poets on both sides of the political spectrum using their craft to comment on contemporary society. Whether they identify as conservatives or liberals, poets engage with the issues of the day—addressing themes such as freedom, justice, identity, and the role of government—and express the growing political chasm that defines much of American life.

This section of this chapter explores how modern poets who identify with conservative and liberal ideologies use poetry to reflect, critique, and express the political and cultural divides in today's America. By examining the works of poets on both ends of the spectrum, we can better understand how poetry becomes a tool for exploring the complexities of belief, values, and political identity in a deeply polarized society.

Conservative Voices in Modern Poetry

Historically, the world of modern poetry has been seen as leaning left, with progressive themes dominating much of the literary conversation. However, there are notable poets who engage with conservative ideals and offer a different perspective on American politics and society. These poets often express themes of tradition, patriotism, individual freedom, and skepticism of government overreach.

Dana Gioia, former Chairman of the National Endowment for the Arts, is an example of a conservative poet who writes about the intersection of politics, culture, and personal values. Gioia's poetry often reflects a deep respect for tradition, emphasizing themes of faith, family, and American cultural heritage. In his poem "The Litany," for instance, Gioia invokes religious tradition and a sense of order that contrasts with the perceived chaos of modern life, expressing a conservative longing for stability and meaning in an increasingly fragmented world.

Gioia's work also reflects conservative critiques of modernity, including concerns about the erosion of community and the weakening of traditional values. His essays on culture frequently touch on the importance of preserving the arts in a way that transcends political partisanship, but with a clear emphasis on cultural continuity and resistance to rapid social change.

Another prominent conservative poet is Robert Bly, who, while often more centrist, engages with themes that resonate with conservative ideologies, particularly in his reflections on masculinity and tradition. Bly's collection Iron John: A Book About Men (1990) explores themes of masculinity, rites of passage, and the loss of traditional male roles in society, all of which align with conservative concerns about modern gender roles and the weakening of traditional family structures.

Christian Wiman, a poet with strong religious themes in his work, also reflects a form of conservative thought through his exploration of faith and spirituality. Wiman's poetry often grapples with questions of existentialism, religious devotion, and the search for meaning in a world marked by secularism. His work resonates with readers who value religious tradition as a guiding principle in life, positioning him within a conservative framework that seeks to preserve spiritual and moral values in an increasingly secular society.

Liberal Voices in Modern Poetry

On the other side of the ideological spectrum, many poets who identify as liberals use their work to challenge political power structures, advocate for social justice, and address issues such as racism, gender equality, and environmentalism. These poets often engage directly with current events and are unafraid to critique institutions they see as upholding inequality or suppressing freedoms.

Maya Angelou's poetry deeply relates to many of the themes we have been discussing, such as the legacy of the Civil War, racial injustice, political division, and the broader struggle for freedom and equality. In her famous poem "Still I Rise," Angelou addresses themes of oppression, inequality, and the enduring strength of Black people in the face of systemic racism. Her work speaks directly to the historical and contemporary realities of African Americans, offering a voice to the often unspoken struggles of the marginalized, while also delivering powerful messages of resilience and hope.

Claudia Rankine, as mentioned earlier, is one of the most prominent liberal voices in modern poetry. Her collection Citizen: An American Lyric takes on race and systemic inequality, offering a searing critique of American society's treatment of African Americans. Rankine uses her poetry to confront racial injustice, including police brutality and microaggressions, and her work reflects a liberal call for accountability and change. She often writes about the emotional and psychological impacts of living in a society where racial bias remains ingrained in social structures. Rankine's work not only reflects her political leanings but also serves as a powerful tool for activism and raising awareness.

Adrienne Rich, though she passed in 2012, remains an influential liberal figure in modern poetry. Her poetry and essays advocated for feminist causes, LGBTQ+ rights, and the fight against patriarchal power structures. Rich's work reflected a clear commitment to liberal ideals, particularly her focus on intersectionality and the ways in which race, gender, and class interconnect in systems of oppression. Her poem "Diving into the Wreck" is often read as a feminist exploration of the need to uncover and address historical wrongs, resonating with ongoing struggles for equality.

Terrance Hayes, another liberal voice, uses his poetry to reflect on the challenges of living in a divided America. In American Sonnets for My Past and Future Assassin, Hayes addresses the political turbulence surrounding race and identity in the U.S., particularly in the aftermath of the 2016 presidential election. His sonnets explore the tensions between personal and national identity, confronting the rise of political extremism and racial violence. Hayes' poetry is marked by a desire to reconcile these divisions, even as he acknowledges the deep ideological and cultural gaps that define modern American life.

The Expression of the Political Divide in Today's Poetry

Whether conservative or liberal, modern poets use their work to express the political divide in America, often reflecting the anxieties, hopes, and frustrations of a nation grappling with profound ideological cleavages. Conservative poets may emphasize themes of tradition, faith, and personal responsibility, while liberal poets focus on justice, equality, and the critique of power structures. Both groups of poets highlight the deep ideological and cultural divisions that define modern American society, but they approach these divisions from different angles—conservatives often seek to preserve or restore, while liberals strive to deconstruct and rebuild. Poetry, in this sense, becomes a battleground for competing visions of what America is and what it should be.

Next Up: Chapter 3: Poetry about Pre-Civil War America, painting a picture of life in the South and North before the Civil War erupted in 1861.

Chapter 3: Pre-Civil War America (Early 1800s-1860)

This chapter's poems delve into the political, social, and economic forces shaping the United States before the Civil War. Several poems explore the rise of slavery as an economic pillar of the South, capturing the voices of enslaved people and abolitionists. The growing abolitionist movement in the North is contrasted with the Southern defense of slavery. These poems examine pivotal moments like the Missouri Compromise, Dred Scott's fateful court decision, and John Brown's raid, bringing to life the emotions, desperation, and ideological divides. Poems also speak to the westward expansion of America, and how the North's industrial ambitions clashed with the agrarian South, intensifying the country's divisions. The growing tensions between regions, as well as the hope for change, are the undercurrents of these poetic reflections.

The divisions between the Northern and Southern colonies of the United States in the pre Civil War era were deeply rooted in the different economic systems, social structures, and political philosophies that had developed since the early colonial period. These differences set the stage for the conflicts that would eventually lead to the Civil War.

Economic Divergence

One of the most significant differences between the Northern and Southern colonies was their economies. The Northern colonies, with their colder climate and rocky soil, developed economies based on small-scale farming, trade, fishing, and industry. By the 19th century, the North had rapidly industrialized, with factories producing textiles, machinery, and other goods. This economic model required wage labor, and there was little reliance on slavery. The growth of commerce and urbanization in the North also led to the development of a more diverse and economically mobile society.

In contrast, the Southern colonies developed an agricultural economy that was deeply reliant on the plantation system. Cash crops like tobacco, rice, and especially cotton became central to the South's economy. The labor-intensive nature of these crops led to a heavy reliance on enslaved African labor, and slavery became an integral part of the Southern economic and social order. By the 19th century, cotton was the dominant crop, driving both the Southern economy and its political interests in preserving and expanding slavery.

Social and Cultural Differences:

The differences in the North and South's economies gave rise to distinct social structures. In the North, a growing middle class of merchants, factory workers, and small farmers supported a society that was more fluid and democratic. The development of public education and widespread literacy in the North also contributed to a culture that placed a high value on civic participation and reform movements, such as abolitionism and women's suffrage.

The Southern colonies, however, developed a rigid, hierarchical society dominated by a small, wealthy class of plantation owners. This elite class controlled both the economy and political life of the South, and their wealth and power were inextricably tied to the institution of slavery. Many Southerners, including poor whites, supported slavery because it was seen as a pillar of social and economic stability, even though most did not own slaves themselves.

Political Philosophies and States' Rights

The Northern and Southern colonies also diverged in their political philosophies. The North increasingly embraced a view of a strong, centralized federal government, particularly after the American Revolution. Northern political leaders tended to support policies that promoted industrial development, infrastructure projects, and tariffs that protected American manufacturing from foreign competition.

The Southern colonies, on the other hand, were staunch advocates of states' rights and a limited federal government. Southern political leaders feared that a strong central government would eventually seek to interfere with slavery. The South's political philosophy was deeply influenced by the need to protect its agrarian economy and the institution of slavery. This focus on states' rights would later be a central argument for Southern secession and the Civil War.

The Role of Slavery

Slavery was the most significant factor that created a chasm between the North and South. While Northern states began to abolish slavery in the late 18th and early 19th centuries, Southern states became more entrenched in the institution, particularly after the invention of the cotton gin in 1793, which made cotton farming far more profitable. By the time of the Civil War, slavery had become not just an economic necessity for the South, but a deeply ingrained social system.

The North's growing abolitionist movement, fueled by religious and moral opposition to slavery, further exacerbated tensions. Northern abolitionists published pamphlets, organized protests, and helped enslaved people escape through the Underground Railroad, all of which infuriated Southern leaders. For the South, slavery was not just an economic institution but a way of life, and they viewed Northern abolitionism as a direct threat to their survival.

Compromise and Conflict

Throughout the first half of the 19th century, the United States attempted to maintain a balance between free and slave states through a series of compromises, such as the Missouri Compromise (1820) and the Compromise of 1850. However, these compromises only delayed the inevitable conflict. The passage of the Fugitive Slave Act and the Kansas-Nebraska Act in the 1850s heightened tensions, as both sides saw their fundamental beliefs being threatened.

Summary

The economic, social, and political differences between the North and South, particularly around the issue of slavery, set the stage for the conflict that would erupt into the Civil War. As the North industrialized and embraced free labor and democracy, the South doubled down on its agrarian, slave-based system and its emphasis on states' rights. These diverging paths made it increasingly difficult for the two regions to coexist within the same nation, ultimately leading to the secession of Southern states and the outbreak of the Civil War in 1861.

Before the Divide

In the years before the battle drums
echoed through divided lands,
before fields were torn by smoke and flame,
there were hearts that held their truths,
as the distance between them deepened.

In the North, they spoke of liberty—
voices rising in crowded streets,
papers rustling with the ink of freedom's dream.
But not all were saints; some hands still clutched profits,
factories built on backs bent low,
turning cotton into gold
without a glance at the hands that picked it.

In the South, there were those who prayed
with calloused palms, eyes cast to heaven,
believing they defended a way of life—
a life rooted deep in the soil,
rich in pride, but blind to chains.

In every town, good and ill walked side by side,
not split by borders or flags,
but by the choices they made,
the truths they refused to see.

And so the rift grew wider,
until words gave way to war,
and both sides would bleed
for what they could not reconcile,
for what they believed was right,
though not all believed justly.

The Roots Beneath the Fire

Beneath the soil of a young nation,
the seeds of conflict took root.
Slavery, states' rights,
the question of freedom,
growing like tangled vines,
thickening through years of compromise.
A wound festering beneath the surface,
waiting for the first crack to spill its blood.

From plantation fields in the South
to the bustling factories of the North,
the divide stretched,
one side bound by chains,
the other tied by a moral thread.
Voices rose in anger,
clashed in Congress,
shouts of liberty and rebellion,
a nation trembling
on the edge of its ideals.

The air grew tense with words,
each louder, heavier,
as if every breath might spark a flame.
Men of power made their choices,
aligning with pride, profit, or principle,
as the nation fractured
not along rivers or mountains,
but within the hearts of men.

Beliefs hardened into weapons,
laws became the battleground.
Each state sought to pull the nation
closer to its will,
until the pressure was too much,
the divide too wide.
And in that moment,
the first shot rang out,
and the nation,
once held together by fragile threads,
began to unravel in fire.

The Cracks in the Foundation

They built this nation on ideals
etched in ink,
freedom, equality, the pursuit of happiness—
but the foundation was laid in soil
that carried the weight of shackled feet.

Each state stood tall,
but not on equal ground.
In the North, they said "progress,"
factories humming with iron and steam,
while the South whispered "tradition,"
hands deep in the cotton fields.

They looked to the future,
but were bound by the past,
and the cracks began to show,
a slow, steady splitting of the ground
between two Americas.

States Draw Their Lines

The line was drawn in invisible ink,
the Mason-Dixon a whisper,
a separation that felt imaginary
until it wasn't.

One by one, they took their stand,
the South with its pride in soil,
its heritage of heat and sweat.
In the North, they called it progress,
pushed their hands into the gears of industry
and watched the South dig deeper into the earth.

States spoke of rights,
of the power to choose—
to own, to oppress, to defy—
but choice was a weapon,
its edges sharp enough
to divide a nation.

The Rising Fire of Belief

In parlors, in halls,
in the streets they gathered—
those who believed in freedom,
and those who wore chains like armor,
afraid to lose the only world they knew.

Words became embers,
heated in the mouths of men,
and every argument was a spark
thrown into the dry grass
of a nation growing more brittle.

They spoke of liberty,
of states and sovereignty,
of a country not made for everyone.
And the fire rose higher,
casting its glow across every state
until the land was ready to burn.

The Election That Broke the Union

When Lincoln stepped into the light,
they saw him not as a man,
but as a force.

One side saw salvation,
the other saw ruin.
It wasn't his words alone,
but the fear they carried,
that made the South tremble.

What would become of their world,
if the man who spoke of freedom
reached too far?

So they left, state by state,
not with a whisper,
but with the loud, cracking sound
of a country breaking apart.

One election, one man,
and the future was written in dust and blood.

Lynching

They left him there,
swinging slow in the still heat,
his toes grazing dirt
like he was trying to come back,
trying to find a foothold.
His hands tied rough,
rope biting into skin
once bound by chains,
but no longer.

The trees were witnesses,
silent and tall,
their shadows long over fields
where his body hung between earth and sky,
a reminder, a warning.

Faces watched,
some with pride,
others with indifference,
but none with shame.
They left him there
to be forgotten,
a name erased,
a soul reduced to silence.

Whippin'

They called it discipline,
but the sound told the truth,
the crack of leather against flesh,
the groans swallowed by dirt.

He thrashed beneath the weight
of cruelty born from fear,
from greed, from the lies they told themselves
about owning another's breath,
about control over someone's pain.

They'd strip the skin if they could,
strip the humanity too,
until nothing but obedience remained,
until the field was quiet
and the cries were buried
under the cotton.

In the Shadow of the Law

In Richmond, Indiana,
beneath the wide Indiana sky,
the Friends gathered, Quakers in quiet stillness,
their faith built on peace,
yet now faced with the weight of a war
waged not with guns, but with hearts torn
between conscience and the law.

It was 1851,
and the fire of freedom burned in hushed corners,
where they sat in a circle,
their simple clothes rustling in the silence,
the air thick with fear and purpose.
Members of the Yearly Meeting of Friends,
bound by something sacred,
spoke of justice,
of chains unseen but felt,
of a path that led to freedom,
and the risk of treading it.

They gathered in a room,
lamplight flickering like their resolve,
whispers barely louder than the ticking of time.
The law had spoken—
the Fugitive Slave Act—
its weight heavy as chains,
dragging even the free into complicity.

"Do we dare?" one voice trembled,
the question hanging like a noose
around the room.
"We must," another answered,
quieter still, but firm,
as though the very walls had ears.

They spoke of paths unseen,
of houses where silence would be kept
and lanterns would signal safety,
where night would swallow the footfalls
of those who fled north
with nothing but hope and terror
in equal measure.

"To defy the law," someone murmured,
"is to risk all—our homes, our families,
our lives."
But then came the counter,
"We are bound by something higher
than any law of man."

The tension hummed like the wind outside,
pushing against the panes,
against the brittle boundaries
of what they knew was right
and what they feared would come
if they were caught.

"God sees what man does not,"
one said, a trembling hand on the Bible.
"We must be the light,
even if it costs us everything."

And so they resolved,
in quiet breaths,
in nods and clasped hands,
to help where they could,
to guide those in darkness
through secret ways
toward the distant promise of freedom,
knowing that in doing so,
they too became fugitives
from the law.

Miscarriage

She was just a girl,
her belly round with hope,
but hope is fragile
in the hands of the indifferent.

The baby never saw light,
never cried,
never drew a breath that was her own.
They said it was nature,
that things happen,
but it wasn't nature that left her alone,
bleeding into the dust
where no doctor's hand would touch her.

She held the baby,
She planned to name Justice,
still and small,
the only sound her whisper
that no one heard.

Playing Marbles

Three white boys crouched in the dust,
the sun high and cruel,
fingers flicking marbles across the ground.
They talked of the heat,
of the work being done for them
by three boys darker than night,
boys the same age,
but different in every way that mattered.

"My daddy's got them breaking their backs,"
one boy said, laughing.
"They ain't fast enough."

Another spat,
"You seen the way they look at us?
Like they don't know their place."

And the marbles rolled,
round and smooth,
as the world spun
and lives broke apart in silence.

Sweet Tea

They sipped slow,
sugar sweet against their lips,
their dresses light as summer air.
The veranda stretched wide,
a place for dreaming,
for whispering about beaus
and dances and the future.

They spoke of the heat,
but not of the ones who worked in it,
who bent low in the fields
while they lifted delicate cups
to their mouths,
oblivious to the hands that picked the leaves,
to the sweat that soaked into the earth.

"Daddy's so kind," one said,
"he lets them rest on Sundays."

And the others nodded,
eyes half-closed
against a world they refused to see,
where sweet tea drowned the truth
and life flowed smooth
for those untouched by it.

The Gathering in Hartford

In a grand room, chandeliers casting
soft light over silverware and crystal goblets,
they gathered,
voices low, conversation clipped
as tension curled between courses.
The clink of forks against porcelain
felt sharper than usual,
cutting through the air thick with thoughts
left unsaid.

Early 1860,
but the year already carried the weight
of something dark on the horizon,
something no one dared name.
They spoke of states, of laws,
of news from the Hartford Courant,
of letters from family,
tales of unrest growing far to the south,
like a storm gathering on distant shores.

One man's voice broke through,
calm yet trembling at the edges—
"Can this end without war?"
And the question lingered,
hovering over the sprawling table,
over glasses half-filled,
over plates left cold.

They all knew, in their hearts,
that the answer had already arrived,
uninvited, unwelcome.
Slavery's shadow could not be lifted
without blood,
without battle.

The future stretched before them
like the untouched dessert,
bitter under the sweetness.

King Cotton

In Wilkinson County,
where the Mississippi sun seared the land,
cotton grew tall and thick,
a sea of white against the scorched earth.
It stretched as far as eyes could see,
fields where backs were broken,
where hands bled raw,
where the sweat of the enslaved
turned into the wealth of men like Joseph Davis.

Brother to Jefferson,
the president of a broken cause,
Joseph knew the currency of cotton—
it was power, it was life,
it was the South's claim to the world.
A crop that built empires,
fed by the blood of those unseen,
those whose names were lost in the rows.

In those fields,
young and old alike,
slaves bent low beneath the weight of King Cotton.
Their bodies bent with the crop,
their spirits crushed beneath the lash,
while the Davises' hands never touched the soil
that made them kings.

Tobacco may have been the South's breath,
but cotton was its heart,
beating with the rhythm of the whip,
driving the Confederacy's engine of war,
funding the fight to preserve a way of life
rooted in chains.

The Davises, the planters,
steadfast in their devotion to this land of cotton,
clung to the lie
that their power would last forever,
that the soil would never turn against them.
The fields murmured a different truth,
each stalk a monument to pain,
where King Cotton sowed a nation's fall.

Mulatto Girl

Born in the cracks of 1845,
where the Antebellum world split
between Black and white,
she came into being—
a shadow on the edge of dusk.
Her skin, neither dark nor light,
held traces from far-off shores,
the salt of Trinidad and Tobago in her veins,
mixed with the blood of slaves
cutting cane under the same sun
that burned her here.

Her bare feet, black as night,
pounded the earth that would never claim her.
They called her witch,
said her green eyes could ensnare
any fool who dared meet her gaze,
eyes as deep as the oceans
that carried her ancestors
from those distant islands.

She was full of secrets,
and her presence lingered
in the fields and the towns,
where no one spoke her name aloud—
not the same name twice.
She was bosomly, filled with something untamed,
her body curving like the hills
that hid things only the darkness knew.
She roamed barefoot on dirt roads,
where children kept their distance,
and men came but never lingered.

Her laugh echoed in the night,
cutting through the silence,
hanging in the air long after
strange things happened—
things no one dared explain.
Some claimed she was cursed,
others believed she brought the curse herself,
but all agreed—
she did not belong in this world.

They feared her,
for she was neither Black nor white,
neither day nor night.
A girl caught in the space between,
rejected by both,
a third world walking among them.
From Trinidad's shores to the deep Southern fields,
she carried histories
like shadows clinging to her skin,
baking under the heat.

She had many names,
depending on who spoke them,
but none fit the way she moved
between the lines of what they knew,
her presence a constant reminder
of a world far more complex,
where she lived and laughed,
untouchable, unclaimed,
half in shadow, half in light.

Through Cotton and Chains

They saw them through clouds of cotton dust,
gentlemen with land as wide as the sky,
and slaves as shadows beneath their feet.
To the North, they were strange aristocrats,
clinging to the old world,
wrapped in the chains they claimed to own,
and their wealth,
grown from hands they did not call their own.

The North saw the South as a contradiction—
free men who lived on stolen lives,
paradise built on backbreaking labor.
They wondered at the pride,
the stubborn roots sunk deep in soil soaked in blood,
and the future—
uncertain, tense,
as if the ground itself would someday crack.

Profiting from the South

They sat in their Northern parlors,
behind polished mahogany and draped curtains,
sipping tea from porcelain cups,
while ships—heavy with cotton—sailed into their ports.
The factories hummed,
spinning the South's bounty into wealth,
while the soil, hundreds of miles away,
soaked up blood and sweat they never felt.

They were Northern aristocrats,
men of commerce, of industry,
their pockets deepened by the hands of slaves
they did not own but surely fed.
In New York, in Boston,
they built their empires on the back of another's labor,
yet never dirtied their hands in the fields.
The contradiction smelled sweet,
like the cotton that filled their looms,
but sour underneath, like a truth no one would name.

They condemned the South's cruelty in public,
their voices loud in abolitionist halls,
yet quietly signed contracts,
imported the very fruits of slavery,
profited from the labor they decried.
They knew the truth but looked away,
blind to the irony,
or too comfortable to care.

In boardrooms they spoke of progress,
of factories and industry,
but their machines were fueled
by the raw power of the South's plantations,
by the hands they pretended were not theirs to control.
They built fortunes on the backs of men,
but called themselves free.

And while they fought for union,
for the promise of a land unbroken by chains,
their mills, their ports, their industries
grew fat on the South's labor.
They preached freedom

and held it close,
yet did not see the chains wrapped around their own wealth,
how their prosperity was born of the same soil
that birthed the Confederacy's pride.

They profited from the very system
they claimed to oppose,
a delicate balance of morality and greed,
a hypocrisy that flourished like cotton in the sun.
And when the war came,
the North still grew rich on the South's suffering,
even as the soldiers marched
and the bodies fell.

The contradictions were not lost,
just ignored,
buried beneath piles of profit,
wrapped in the comfort of distance,
as if the cruelty was not their own.

Slavery

They came in chains,
stripped of their names, their language,
their homes far across the ocean,
most from West Africa,
but others too, swept up
in the endless trade of flesh.
Taken from the land of their ancestors,
to the land called the home of the free,
only to find themselves bound again,
hands bloodied by cotton, tobacco, sugar,
fields stretching out under an unforgiving sun.

They were not seen as human.
They were labor, bodies bought and sold,
counted as property,
stripped of everything but breath.
Owned by men who stood tall in their belief
that skin alone made them worthy
of freedom,
that by birthright alone, they could hold another's fate
in their hands.

Day and night,
bent beneath the weight of the crop
and the lash,
they worked.
The sun burned their backs,
but the heat wasn't the worst of it—
it was the eyes of those who owned them,
who saw them as less,
who thought their humanity could be priced,
their spirit could be broken,
with words that reduced them
to mere tools.

America did this—
the land that called itself just,
the land that prided itself on liberty
allowed 15 states to condone the ownership
of other human beings.
Hatred thrived in those places,
growing alongside the crops.

Bigotry had deep roots
that reached down into the soil,
nurtured by the belief
that white was right,
that whiteness alone gave the right to be free.

And the owners,
they capitalized on every lash,
every bead of sweat,
turning labor into gold,
turning men and women into wealth.
They lived in comfort,
while the enslaved lived in chains,
two lives connected by the same cruel thread
of power and control.

To be a slave,
to wake each day in darkness,
to feel the weight of ownership
in every moment,
and to know there would be no escape—
that was the reality.
To be an owner,
to profit from pain,
to justify every act of cruelty with a system
designed to protect it—
that was the other side of the same coin.

We did these things in America.
We built our wealth on their backs,
we let the hatred grow,
we told ourselves some were less human,
less deserving of breath,
and let the lie become the truth.

Next Up: Chapter 4, Civil War America: The Nation at War, which focuses on the chaos and brutality of battle, showing America's transformation from a unified nation to one engulfed in violent struggle. The battles and personal conflicts reflect the war's ferocity.

Chapter 4: Civil War America (1861-1865)

The war that tore through America in the 1860s was not just a conflict between two opposing sides—it was a confrontation that exposed the nation's fragile foundation, revealing that true unity had always been elusive. America, a land built on diverse ideas and identities, had long accepted differences if those differences did not violate basic human rights or the law. However, the stark division over slavery shattered this uneasy balance, transforming ideological conflicts into violent battles. Men from both the North and the South marched into the chaos of war with unwavering convictions, but also with trepidation about the unknown future. The thunder of cannons echoed across fields stained with blood, and the cries of the wounded filled the air. Each clash of arms was a harsh reminder of how quickly ideals can devolve into brutality when the basic rights and dignity of others are at stake. The nation, never fully unified, splintered further, with families torn apart, cities reduced to ashes, and lives lost in the name of causes both righteous and tragic.

As the war raged on, the battlefield became a stage where personal conflicts mirrored the larger struggle. Brothers fought against brothers, and friends became enemies, with each side believing in the righteousness of their cause. The Union fought to preserve the nation, to hold together the fragile threads of democracy, while the Confederacy fought for what they saw as their right to independence and way of life. Yet, amid this grand clash of principles, the individual toll was immense—young soldiers who once dreamed of glory were torn apart, both physically and emotionally, by the relentless violence. As the smoke from muskets and cannons filled the sky, the country was left torn and tattered, its heart scarred by the brutality of a war that would forever reshape its identity.

War should always be a last resort, and the same must be said of violence, as both call into question the very essence of our humanity. Though America has made significant strides toward becoming a more inclusive, equitable, and free society, our journey is far from complete. We must continue to reject conflict and violence in all forms, striving instead for dialogue and understanding as we work to fulfill the promise of a truly just and united nation.

A Nation Divides: November 6, 1860

It began in the crisp air of November,
as the country held its breath,
caught between the rising sun and the gathering storm.
Lincoln's name rose and fell in the streets,
a tall figure from Illinois,
whose words spoke of unity,
but whose election cracked the very ground beneath them.

The North saw hope that morning,
the sky clear, the streets bustling,
newspapers fluttering with headlines:
"Lincoln Elected!"
His victory painted on every page,
a triumph for those who believed the Union must hold,
who whispered of a future where no man owned another.

But the South—
oh, the South felt the chill of something deeper than winter.
The weather was no colder than usual,
but hearts shivered at the news,
the headlines in Richmond and Charleston darkened,
"The Black Republican Wins," they hissed.
The mood, tense and taut, like a rope pulled too tight,
a nation poised on the edge of breaking.

Lincoln had defeated men with names like Bell,
Breckinridge, and Douglas,
faces that could have kept the peace,
so the South believed.
But it was the rail-splitter, the lawyer,
the one who spoke of a house divided
who rose above them all.

In the North, factory whistles sang with joy,
the streets rang with the clatter of horses,
as men in top hats and woolen coats hurried to tell the news.
But in the South, men stared at the horizon,
silent, knowing what was coming.
The day had been clear, but the future—
the future was clouded,
and all could see that this moment was the first step toward war.

The votes were counted,
the decision made,
and though no cannon had yet fired,
the echoes of war already rippled through the land.
On that November day,
Lincoln took his place—
not as a beacon of triumph,

Incipit

Morning cracks with cannon fire,
the sky over Charleston darkens,
a storm of iron and smoke rising from the sea.
Fort Sumter stands,
its brick walls trembling,
caught in the crosshairs of history.

Inside, men move in shadows,
fingers blistered on cold metal,
their faces lit by the brief flare of muzzle flash.
They fight, not for victory,
but to hold the impossible,
to keep a flag fluttering
in a sky that has forgotten peace.

The harbor echoes with the roar of a divided nation,
its voice carried by every blast
that slams into Sumter's stone skin.
The walls crack but do not fall—not yet.

Fire and ash swirl,
the air choked with what was once brick,
once calm,
once whole.

For thirty-four hours, the world narrows,
becomes this island,
this moment—
an end, but also a beginning.

Incipit,
they call it in Latin,
the first note in a symphony of war,
where no one dies today,
but the earth trembles with what is to come.

At dawn, surrender—
not of spirit,
but of stone and flame.
The flag comes down,
and with it, a nation rises to war.
but as the fulcrum upon which the fate of a nation would turn.

A Blur of Color

On the fields of Manassas,
July 21, 1861,
the sun rose to witness a war
where men marched, not in ranks of blue and gray,
but in a storm of colors.
Blue coats clashed with gray,
but who could tell them apart
in the haze of gunfire,
the earth trembling beneath a tide of confused uniforms?

Farm boys from Virginia stood in blue,
city men from New York in gray,
brothers in arms, now faceless figures
lost in a dance of smoke and flame.
Red-trousered Zouaves,
their bright uniforms glowing,
rushed into the fray,
their fezzes bouncing with each step—
as if this were a carnival,
and not the bloody work of war.

Artillery thundered,
minié balls screamed through the air,
and still the question rose—
friend or foe?
The colors betrayed them,
tricked them into firing on their own,
into retreating, advancing,
and retreating again.

Chaos swallowed the day,
as the lines crumbled,
and the field became a blur of bodies and fabric,
of fear and valor,
of uniforms that meant nothing,
only the smoke,
only the blood,
only the roar of war's first cry.

By dusk, the field lay silent, colors fading into night.
Soldiers learned that war doesn't care what you wear,
only that you bleed.

John Calvin Barrett

Born in the hills of Monroe County,
Ohio—1846,
before the country was torn apart.
Grandma couldn't say much,
she didn't know his stories,
but I can feel them—
etched into the soil of Grandview Township,
just upriver from Marietta.

He wore Union blue,
young, but old enough to know
what war does to a man.
He marched to Camp Chase,
mustered in as the winter winds howled,
February of '65—
too late for glory,
but not too late to feel the weight of duty.

To Nashville, Chattanooga,
the train tracks and the bridges—
guarding what connected North and South,
the Tennessee River flowing beneath his feet
like the bloodlines of a broken nation.
Rebel cavalry lurked in the brush,
guerrillas striking like shadows,
but it wasn't the bullets that haunted him—
it was the nights,
cold and unrelenting.

He came home in one piece,
but his body carried more than it should.
Exposure to war's bitter elements,
the damp nights of the South,
settling into his bones,
the weight of silence
when the skirmishes had passed.
Anxiety, they called it,
but it was more—
the kind of burden you carry
when you've seen the cost of holding a bridge
that spans more than just rivers.

By the time he laid down his rifle,
Edgefield was quiet,
the rebellion beaten but still echoing.
September came,
and with it, the mustering out—
back to Camp Chase,
back to Ohio.
But home,
home had shifted beneath his feet.

John Calvin Barrett,
my great-great-grandfather,
came back to the hills
with stories unsaid,
but I hear them in the wind,
feel them in the earth,
and see them in the eyes of men
who've known too much of war.

Purse and Puppet String Holders

In shadowed rooms and quiet halls,
they shifted coins, not soldiers,
across the war's chessboard.

Jay Cooke sold bonds like bread,
feeding the Union's hunger for men and bullets.
Vanderbilt's iron tracks stretched like veins,
carrying soldiers, unsure if they'd return.

Forbes and Belmont, bankers with quills,
held the war by its purse,
while Southern planters wove fortunes into cotton,
their empire bound to the backs of the enslaved.

Judah Benjamin, sharp-eyed and silver-tongued,
whispered across oceans,
pleading for foreign gold and ships that never came.

The Cotton Lobby, calling itself King,
watched its thread unravel,
as Europe turned away.

Copperheads hissed from Northern shadows,
Vallandigham's voice urging peace,
even as the war devoured all.

And Thurlow Weed, the master of spin,
played the public like tops,
his deals hidden beneath Washington's tablecloths.

Profiteers in gray and blue fed on the war's carcass,
selling cloth for shrouds and guns for killing.

The Rothschilds, silent across the sea,
felt the weight of their gold in both pockets,
their power unseen but pulling at the seams of both sides.

They spun their webs too tight,
and when the war ended,
they too were caught,
while soldiers fell like puppets,
their strings cut by the final shot, and silence.

Wartime Men of God

God was there,
on both sides of the Mason-Dixon,
slipping through pulpits and pews.

In Plymouth Church, Beecher thundered,
God cloaked in abolition,
nodding at hymns of freedom
while Conway pointed runaway souls North.

But down South,
God wore chains in Dabney's sermons,
righteousness laced with rebellion,
while "Fighting Bishop" Polk swapped the cross for a sword,
marching through Dixie's dust.

Gunpowder and psalms filled the night air,
as Palmer preached fire,
and God cast His shadow over bent backs
in cotton fields stained with sweat.

Up North, Phillips Brooks stood tall,
a beacon in the chaos,
while God hummed along,
playing both sides,
letting truth and war tangle.

In Confederate gray, Bannon prayed,
God whispered to soldiers,
each caught in history's snare.

Yes, God was there,
in every sermon, every shot,
good and evil spun tight together—
letting the nation choose
which thread would snap first.

Wheeling, West Virginia, 1861

The Ohio River runs dark with the weight of divided homes,
its current winding through fields where iron bends to cannon
and salt feeds the war machine.

Wheeling stands as a gateway,
not just to the North,
but to the spirit of a place torn between itself.
Some men take up arms for the Union,
while others, silent in the night,
slip away with the Shriver Grays,
southward to fight for a cause
that grips their hearts, if not their neighbors'.

The mills hum, turning iron into power,
the smell of coal thick in the valley air.
A state is born not from peace,
but from fracture,
Wheeling's streets echo with the sound of horses,
the hurried steps of men bound for war.

In the mountains, the battles rage,
Rich Mountain, Carnifex Ferry—
blood on unfamiliar soil.
Yet back home,
the clatter of industry drowns out the fear,
forging steel and resolve in equal measure.

Fathers watch as their sons march east,
not knowing which flag they'll raise
when they return,
or if they'll return at all.

Chagrin Falls, Ohio During the Civil War

Have you walked to the Civil War Memorial
on Evergreen Hill, where names stand still,
etched in silence against the wind's chill?

Boys from Chagrin—farmers, millhands,
marching to battlefields they'd never seen.
Gettysburg, Chattanooga, Big Creek—
unknown until their blood named them.

A village of 1,200 sent over 200.
Brothers, friends, side by side,
in the 23rd OVI, the 103rd OVI,
the Ohio Cavalry—boys turned soldiers, turned memory.

At home, women stitched through fear,
meeting weekly. Jane Church kept the lists—
who brought bandages, who gave their coin,
who waited in quiet dread.

Letters came back, but not all boys did.
Twenty-one lost, some starved in Andersonville,
never to return.

The village raised $1,350
for a stone to speak their names,
to stand against the wind,
a pillar of sorrow and strength.

The mills still turned,
life kept moving,
but the war weighed heavy—
uncertain futures held close by those who stayed behind.

The monument stands, even now,
overlooking a village that remembers—
not just the names,
but the lives that shaped this place.

Homecoming

Four years gone,
he walked the road,
a shadow of the man he was.
The South lay in ruins,
and so did he—
broken, body and soul.

No letters, no word,
just three years in a Union prison,
haunted by fifty lives he took
with a single bomb.
Now, the house still stood,
and the boy—
his son,
born while he was away—
ran to meet him,
eyes bright with life.

The word "Daddy"
cut through the silence.
He couldn't meet the boy's gaze,
afraid of what he'd see.
But the boy smiled,
and somehow,
in that smile,
he found a way home.

Nobody Knew How Long It Would Last

They thought it would be over
by the harvest,
before the leaves turned red
and fell like soldiers
cut down in fields.
But the war stretched on—
an endless line of boots
marching toward a horizon
that never came.

Nobody knew how long it would last.
They counted days
like grains of corn in a sack,
hoping the supply would hold,
but the sacks emptied,
the land turned barren,
and the sky offered no relief.

Letters came less often,
ink smudged by rain and blood.
Mothers buried the words
before they buried their sons.
In towns where the church bells
once rang for Sunday services,
now they tolled for the dead—
their echoes carried by the wind
like a distant thunder
no one could escape.

The fields stayed unplowed,
as farmers traded plows for rifles,
hands calloused by work
became hands that shook
under the weight of war.
Every hill, every river,
every fence line became a border
between life and loss.

The truth was,
they didn't care how long it lasted—
as long as the other side broke first,
as long as they could stand and say,

"We won."

But the war didn't listen
to pride or purpose.
It devoured both
and left only bones
where dreams had been.

Still, they fought on,
because what else could they do
but fight
until there was nothing left to fight for,
until the last cannon fired,
until surrender
was the only thing left to give.

Nobody knew how long it would last—
all they knew
was it would last
as long as it took
for someone to finally say
they'd lost.

The Trent Affair, 1861

On the cold waters off Cuba,
a Union ship cut through the salt and wind,
its captain with eyes sharp, his purpose clear—
to seize what he could not allow to cross the Atlantic.
Two men, bound for Europe,
carried more than themselves;
they carried a cause,
a Confederacy seeking the world's ear.
Mason and Slidell—envoys of rebellion—
snatched from the deck of the Trent,
as if their words could tip the scales of war,
as if diplomacy were cannon fire.

Across the sea, Britain's temper flared,
a proud nation insulted; its ship violated.
A breach of law, a breach of pride—
outrage boiled in London's halls.
Sovereignty at stake, they said.
An apology demanded,
their armies readied for conflict,
their ships prepared for retaliation.
A war beyond American shores
teetered on the edge of a word,
on the bow of a ship in foreign waters.

In Washington, Lincoln listened to the storm,
to the rising winds from across the Atlantic.
The Union already fractured, already bleeding—
another war could rip it further apart.
And so he let the prisoners go,
not out of weakness, but wisdom.
Captain Wilkes had acted on his own, they claimed,
his fervor not their command.
Better to swallow pride
than to face British guns and diplomatic collapse.

Mason and Slidell continued their voyage,
though Europe's doors would stay closed to their cause.
The Confederacy's hopes slipped with each wave,
as Britain, neutral and watchful,
remained on the sidelines of a war
that threatened to engulf them.

In the end, it was not battle that decided fate,
but diplomacy, that fragile thread
that held the world from spiraling into flame.

The seas calmed,
but the lesson remained—
a nation torn from within
could not afford to provoke another storm.
In those moments,
on a ship, in a decision,
the future hung in the balance,
and restraint,
not fury, carried the day.

Battle of Shiloh, April 6-7, 1862

Before the shots,
Shiloh was just a church,
a quiet place
where hymns rose softly
and the trees murmured prayers
over the river.

Then the storm came—
a clash unexpected,
men swallowed by fear,
the ground trembling
beneath their boots.

Day one—chaos,
lines shattered,
soldiers tempted to run,
to leave the field
to the dead.
Bullets hissed
through the Hornet's Nest,
stinging skin,
breaking spirit.

Day two—
the Union pushed,
Confederates fell back,
victory claimed
on ground soaked red.

Shiloh, once a haven,
now a grave.
They left it behind,
but no one walked.

The Blind Cotton Picker

He felt the sun,
not by its light,
but by its weight on his back.
The cotton fields stretched,
an endless sea he couldn't see,
but his fingers knew every row,
cracked and bleeding
from years of pulling white
from thorned branches.

His grandson led him,
whispering, "Here, Gran'papa,"
his small hands guiding large rough ones.
The cotton cut deep,
but the master demanded more—
always more.

His daughter worked beside him,
silent, her pain buried
beneath the snap of the whip.
At night, in the dark they shared,
he knew her tears fell
like the rain that never came.

Gran'papa worked faster,
by touch, not sight.
His hands knew the burrs,
the chains he couldn't break.
He stumbled once,
the boy too small to catch him,
but enough to keep him standing.
In the fields, there were no stars,
only darkness,
the sound of cotton torn from its roots,
like his life,
slowly ripped away
by hands too tired to fight.

Second Battle of Bull Run

At Bull Run's fields, Lee took his stand,
With Jackson's might and Longstreet's hand.
Pope's Union forces, proud and tall,
Were no match for the South's fierce call.

They flanked, they charged, they fought as one,
And soon the Union came undone.
Through dust and smoke, the battle raged,
But Lee's bold plan could not be caged.

With every turn, the South gained ground,
The Union's hopes were quickly drowned.
As night fell down, the battle won,
The Northern troops were forced to run.

This victory set Lee's path ahead,
But in its wake, so many dead.
The South would cheer, but soon they'd know,
That war's true cost is bitter woe.

The Battle of New Orleans, April 25-May 1, 1862

They came with the river,
the Union fleet,
ironclads cutting through the waters
like silent knives.
The Mississippi roared,
its muddy banks trembling
beneath the weight of warships
carrying the end of a city's pride.

New Orleans,
sweet with magnolia blooms
and the song of riverboats,
braced itself.
Cannons barked from Fort Jackson,
Fort St. Philip,
but the ironclads moved like ghosts,
shaking off the fire,
pressing forward.

The people watched from rooftops,
from alleyways,
feeling the ground shudder
with each blast,
hearts heavy with fear.
The air smelled of gunpowder and salt,
but also of something more—
the sour stench of surrender
before the first white flag was raised.

The city had never seen its death
coming like this.
Behind the palmettos and oaks,
men cursed and prayed,
their fingers clenched around rifles
that never fired a shot.
They felt the helplessness,
the weight of defeat sinking in
before a single soldier set foot
on their soil.

The sounds of war grew closer,
but inside,

there was only silence.
A stillness that spread,
like the fog over the bayou at dawn,
choking the spirit
that once danced in the streets.
Confederate hopes crumbled
in the face of the inevitable,
a quiet collapse of a city too proud
to imagine this end.

When the Union soldiers arrived,
they found no fight,
just a city waiting,
already surrendered in its heart.
Flags came down—
not with fanfare,
but with a sigh.
New Orleans was taken
without the glory of battle,
without the roar of rebellion,
just the slow folding
of a city's soul
into the river that had always
carried its fate.

Victory for the North,
defeat for the South,
but in the streets,
it felt like something more—
the end of an era,
the drowning of a dream
in the deep, muddy waters
of the Mississippi.

Chancellorsville: A Divided Triumph

Lee looked out over the wilderness,
a sea of trees thick with uncertainty,
outnumbered, outgunned,
but never outwitted.

He divided them,
sent Stonewall to flank,
a move bold as thunder,
lightning flashing in the eyes
of an unsuspecting Union.
The forest swallowed their steps,
until they were there—
a storm crashing down
on Hooker's men.
Confusion broke their ranks,
and the once mighty Union
was driven back,
the roar of cannon
fading in retreat.

Victory tasted of iron,
but Jackson fell,
not by the hands of the enemy,
but by his own,
a shadow crossing the sun
on that blood-soaked ground.
And so, the South stood victorious,
but hollow,
for the arm that struck with such force
would never rise again.
Lee knew what was lost
amid the triumph.
Chancellorsville,
a field of both glory
and grief.

War Feeds on Itself

War feeds on itself,
never sated, never done.
Life spills, hearts break,
and still, it marches on.

It consumes the fallen,
drinks the tears,
swallows hope,
devours years.

Marches on, still.
And hearts break, life spills.
Never done, never sated—
war feeds on itself.

The Paperwork of War

Records kept in ink and dust,
names of battles, dates of loss.
Each injury tallied, every trust,
on paper marked by blood and cost.

Plans drawn with trembling hands,
strategies shaped by hurried minds.
The numbers told where armies stand,
death and tolls in silent lines.

Both sides wrote what they believed,
sent to papers for all to see—
victory claimed, or hope deceived,
in words that outlived history.

The Nightmares of a Broken Soldier

He wakes in sweat, the battle near,
his leg long gone, but the pain remains.
The screams of men still pierce his ear,
his body battered, filled with stains.

His wife beside him, soft and still,
whispers comfort through the dark,
but no words can calm the chill
of memories that leave their mark.

Some nights he drinks at the saloon,
lost in whiskey, lost in thought,
the days are blurred beneath the moon,
but peace is something never caught.

The nightmares come, and then he's gone—
one final step, no more to fight.
His wife found him with the dawn,
the war still raging in his night.

The War That Wore No Uniforms

They fought with silence,
beneath the sky,
a war of susurrus,
as clouds rolled by.
Not bullets, but glances,
in parlors where lace curtains
held the air.

In kitchens, in fields,
it wasn't rifles
that made the din,
but waiting, watching,
secrets kept,
as soldiers passed
and towns slept.

It was the war of letters burned,
of songs unsung,
the war that wore no uniforms,
yet stained every heart the same.

Not a monument stands for it,
but you've seen it—
in the pause before you speak,
the tear you swallow,
the light you seek.

The General's Shoes

They polished his boots
until they gleamed like stars,
but no one noticed
the soles worn thin
from pacing floors at night.

He gave the orders,
sharp as bayonets,
and they followed with pride,
yet his own heart trembled,
uncertain of its compass.

Maps spread wide
across tables of oak,
he traced the lines with a finger
steady as steel,
though his dreams ran in circles,
chasing ghosts of home.

They speak of his strategy,
his brilliance,
his name etched in stone—
but never of the moments
his breath caught in his chest,
wondering if his hands
had led too many
into darkness.

His medals shine
in museum cases,
but his boots—
those tired, silent boots—
lie forgotten
beneath the glass,
still caked with the mud
of battlefields
where nothing ever grows.

He walks through history
with a straight back, yet you'd never guess
how those boots ached to turn around
and run.

The Last Letter Home

He never sent the letter
folded tight in his coat,
ink smudged by rain
and trembling hands.
It spoke of harvests
never gathered,
of a daughter's laugh
that echoed in dreams
but never reached his ears.

He wrote of fields,
not the ones soaked in blood,
but the golden waves
he left behind,
the smell of earth
before the plow.

The paper, brittle now,
carried no grand ideas of victory
or flags unfurled,
just the simple hope
that someone might remember
the sound of his name
in the quiet morning air.

He never sent it—
no grand reason why.
Maybe he feared
that if he wrote it down,
it would mean the end.
Instead, it rested with him,
close to his heart,
as he lay down
beneath the sky,
where all things
return to silence.

The war went on without him.
The fields grew wild.
And somewhere,
a daughter laughed, unaware that
he had listened one last time.

The Numbers Don't Tell It All

Over 10,000 times
the soldiers clashed—
North against South,
blue against gray,
on blood-soaked fields,
in tangled forests,
under blistering skies,
through biting cold.

10,000 times they fought,
but the numbers
don't tell the whole story.
Yes, there were 200 Union victories,
and 100 for the Confederates,
but most of those battles
faded like whispers,
lost in the chaos of war.

It was not the skirmishes,
not the small engagements
that decided a nation's fate.
It was the ones
that roared like thunder,
the battles where hope rose
and crumbled in a single breath.

Gettysburg—
where the ground turned red,
where Southern dreams broke
under the weight of Northern resolve.
A single clash,
a turning point,
a battlefield that echoed
with the end of Confederate glory.

Vicksburg—
where the Mississippi ran thick
with loss,
as the Union split the South in two,
and victory tightened its grip
on a fractured land.

These battles,
more than all the rest,
shifted the course of history.
Though the South had its victories,
it was the North's endurance,
its relentless supply of men,
of iron and railroads,
that wore the Confederacy down.

In the end, it wasn't just numbers—
not the 10,000 skirmishes,
not the 100 victories—
but the few decisive moments
that decided the war.

And with those victories came loss.
Confederate soldiers, 258,000 dead,
a staggering toll of men,
lost to bullets, bayonets,
disease that crept silently
through camps.
Union soldiers, 365,000 dead,
not just in battle,
but in hospital tents
where fevers claimed as many
as rifles ever could.

Numbers cannot speak of sorrow.
They do not tell
of wives left behind,
of children who waited for fathers
who never returned.
The South, though fierce,
bled itself dry,
until Richmond fell—
not with a roar,
but with the slow crumble of hope.

The war wasn't won
in the 10,000 minor clashes,
but in the few,
the pivotal,
where fate stood still

and chose a side.
In the end,
the numbers are vast,
but they will never speak
of the full weight of loss.

After the Battle in the Wilderness

The field lay torn,
scarred by war,
but today the sun was soft,
its light a quiet balm
on the broken ground.

A breeze rustled
through the groans of fallen men,
their pain fading into the air,
while the bluebells at the forest's edge
bloomed,
small and defiant,
unaware of the death around them.
Spring had returned,
though no one could say
what season lived in the hearts
of the dead.

The land, breathing again,
remembered life,
as the bluebells swayed gently,
unmoved by battle,
standing in quiet victory
over the violence
that had passed through.

New Market's Forgotten Corners

In New Market, where grasses swayed,
And the mist of dawn refused to fade,
There lay a place, away from fame,
Where silence ruled, and shadows came.

No generals stood to give commands,
No flags were waved by trembling hands.
Here, beneath the darkened sky,
Were murmurs of the boys who'd die.

A barn stood still, its roof half torn,
Its fields now trampled, not with corn,
But boots abandoned in the rain,
Where soldiers fell and left their pain.

The Shenandoah's waters bled,
A slow, dark stream, a crimson thread,
Where rifles broken kissed the ground,
And cadet caps, now lost, were found.

A lone shoe dangled from a tree,
Swaying gently in the breeze,
Telling tales of a boy who cried
For home, before he closed his eyes.

The crows watched with their weary wings,
Above the wreck of human things.
They croaked a song no ears could bear,
A hymn of sorrow in the air.

Yet through the fields of death and strife,
Wildflowers clung to stubborn life,
Their petals soft as soldiers' breath,
A fragile beauty born from death.

New Market, in pages turned,
Is fire and blood, the lessons learned,
But in its cracks, in shadowed light,
Lie smaller stories, lost to sight.

One End, Another Beginning

The guns grew quiet on fields of strife,
Where once the clash of war had reigned.
The smoke had lifted, sparing life,
Yet in its wake, so much remained.

The battle-torn ground, now cold and still,
Held stories of the lives it claimed.
For every victory, there was a kill,
And every heart was left untamed.

The papers signed, the war was done,
But what had truly been repaired?
A fractured land beneath the sun,
With wounds too deep to be declared.

Lincoln spoke of healing fast,
Yet in the South, resentment grew.
The North had triumphed—but that would pass,
As shadows lingered, dark and true.

Reconstruction came, but walls were high,
And freedom's promise hard to find.
The chains were gone, but so was the sky,
And hope was slow, and justice blind.

What led to peace was weary souls,
The cost too great, too high, too deep.
The rivers swelled beyond control,
And ghosts would haunt the land they'd keep.

But even in the ash and flame,
The seeds of something new would rise.
Though torn apart, we'd bear the shame,
And strive again beneath new skies.

For every war must end in grief,
Yet from the loss, new strength can bloom.
The Civil War was sharp, not brief,
Its echoes linger in our gloom.

Next Up: Post-Civil War America (1865-1899): While history books say
the Civil War ended in 1865, that is the farthest thing from the truth.

Chapter 5: Post-Civil War America (1865-1899)

Post-Civil War America was a period of profound transformation but also of missed opportunities, as the country struggled to rebuild itself while grappling with unresolved tensions over race, labor, and economic power. Reconstruction offered an unprecedented chance to reimagine the South and integrate formerly enslaved people into society as equal citizens. The passage of the 13th, 14th, and 15th Amendments sought to enshrine these rights, formally abolishing slavery, granting citizenship, and ensuring voting rights for African American men. However, these gains were fleeting, as the rise of Jim Crow laws, segregation, and the violent resurgence of white supremacy—embodied by groups like the Ku Klux Klan—sabotaged these efforts. Many white Southerners resisted change, using violence, intimidation, and discriminatory laws to reassert control and maintain racial hierarchy.

Politically empowered African Americans were swiftly disenfranchised through voter suppression tactics like literacy tests, poll taxes, and grandfather clauses, which ensured that the promise of true equality remained unfulfilled. Economically, the South's structure remained largely unchanged, as sharecropping and tenant farming systems replaced slavery, yet kept Black Americans and poor whites trapped in cycles of debt and poverty. Reconstruction collapsed, and with it, the chance for a more just society in the South.

Meanwhile, the North experienced a different transformation. It embraced industrial capitalism, with the expansion of railroads, steel production, and factories marking America's shift into modernity. Cities grew rapidly, attracting waves of immigrants and laborers seeking work in these new industries. However, the Gilded Age, as it came to be known, was a time of both great wealth and deep inequality. While industrialists like Andrew Carnegie and John D. Rockefeller amassed immense fortunes, the working class struggled with poor working conditions, long hours, and minimal wages. Labor strikes and movements, like the Great Railroad Strike of 1877, reflected growing discontent among workers who felt they were being exploited by the powerful industrialists.

The political landscape of the Gilded Age was rife with corruption, as political machines and patronage systems thrived, often serving the interests of the wealthy rather than the general population. The disparity between the wealthy elite and the impoverished working class echoed unresolved tensions about who would truly benefit from America's newfound prosperity. Although the Civil War had ended, the nation continued to grapple with deep divisions—whether racial, economic, or social—that would persist for decades to come.

In the end, both the North and the South faced challenges in the post-war period. In the South, it was a failure to fully dismantle the institution of white supremacy and create an equitable society for all its citizens. In the North, it was a question of whether the economic gains of industrialization could be shared more broadly, or if the new wealth would remain in the hands of a few, perpetuating cycles of inequality and unrest. Both regions missed key opportunities to build a more inclusive and just America, laying the groundwork for struggles that would continue well into the 20th century.

Reconstruction in Georgia, 1866

They ride again, not as they once did—
gray coats gone, but their hearts still
weighted by defeat.

In the dust-clouded dawn,
they gather in silence,
eyes fixed on the road
where Union men—strangers—
bring new laws,
new roads,
new names
to the county they once called theirs.

The plow rusts, idle,
under the shadow
of an unfamiliar flag.

"What can you rebuild,"
they murmured
beneath the oak's ancient limbs,
"when the roots of this land
still remember the war?"

Widows of Greensboro, 1865

They gather beneath the wide, flat sky,
skirts dusted with the red earth
of Greensboro, Alabama,
three months since the last shot
rang out, but still,
no word from the men they love.

Each day the road is the same—
a silent stretch
until a shuffle of feet, a flash of gray.
Soldiers return,
limping, broken, but whole enough to embrace.
For some, joy springs—
a father's weary grin, a son's tight arms.
For others,
there is only emptiness
as the sun sets without a single step.

The Great Mobile Hurricane, 1865

The war had ended,
but peace came with no calm.

In September, the storm arrived
like another siege—
buildings already weak from cannon fire
crumbled under winds no man could fight.

The harbor swelled,
swallowed ships like secrets,
while the streets of Mobile
filled with water, fear, and confusion.

Men, tired of fighting, rebuilt in the rain,
but the war wasn't done with them—
nor was the earth.

Now it was the wind's turn,
to tear what little remained
of hope, of home.

The Cottonwood Never Learned

It was 1867 and the fields lay fallow,
waiting for a labor force that no longer
could be owned. The townspeople watched
from behind lace curtains, from broken porches
where the wood still smelled of gunpowder.

And the freedmen built cabins
at the edge of the cotton fields
under the low-leaning branches
of trees that never heard a sermon.

They planted turnips, sweet corn
and waited, waited for something
more than mere survival—
for promises to root
in the dirt where the graves
of their fathers
lay covered with wild tobacco.

In town, a preacher's son had learned
to spell emancipation before he knew
the word meant
to lose everything—he watched
his father stare at the Bible,
its pages pale as the ghost
of a lost war, pale
as the face of his mother
who told him there was no place
for mercy in Mississippi.

The freedmen held meetings
in the shadow of cottonwoods,
where they spoke of dreams they dared
never say to their wives, of wages
earned and the distant hope
of their own land, the laughter
of children who never knew
the crack of a whip.

The preacher's son, seventeen
and tired of hollow sermons,
walked to the clearing, offered his hands,

and no one spoke
as he picked up an axe
and began to split wood for cabins.
The air between them was thick,
a question no one asked aloud:
Could the preacher's son be trusted,
this boy who smelled of ink and fear,
whose father spat words
like curses from his pulpit?

And yet—
he stayed. He built cabins
in the low, swampy ground,
and his mother looked on from her porch,
the sky above her turning
bruise-purple, the horizon filled
with men who refused
to believe in change.

When night fell, the preacher's son sat
by a fire he did not build, drank corn whiskey
offered by a man named Solomon,
who spoke in low tones of a brother
taken by the river, who spoke
of a hope that was not yet dead—
though it was tired, so tired
from carrying too many bones.

The preacher's son listened,
and as the fire cracked,
and the voices of men lingered
in the branches of trees that had seen
too much hate—
the cottonwood never learned
the words of forgiveness—
he knew his hands would carry this weight
forever, and that maybe
the only grace
was in knowing it.

Walk to Freedom

From Tuscaloosa's broken land,
They packed their dreams and walked away,
No longer bound by iron hand,
But freedom's road was hard each day.

The scars of war still marked the South,
Yet hope now spread from Indiana's shore,
With quiet plans and word of mouth,
They journeyed north to start once more.

Through fields of cotton, long left wild,
And rivers deep that ran with pain,
They carried hope for every child,
To leave behind the South's dark chain.

To Madison, where freedom called,
Across the land of broken men,
They built their lives where none could fall,
And never feared those chains again.

The road was long, but hearts were light,
For once the shackles lay undone,
They found their peace in morning's bright,
And walked toward a rising sun.

Rise of the Klan

Out of Tennessee's ashes,
from the bones of a dying war,
they rise, cloaked—
not in honor, but in secrecy,
not in glory, but in shadow,
riders who come in the night.

Pulaski, it was,
they say, the cradle,
where former soldiers, their uniforms buried,
took up new flags.
Nathan Bedford Forrest, they whisper,
the man with the general's eyes,
carved a different battlefield—
no drums, no bugles, only
whip cracks and silent torches.
December, 1865, when it all began.

Some call it defense,
protection for a South burned raw,
skin torn from the land
by an army of men who never knew
cotton or tobacco,
only iron rails and wages.
The Appeal writes,
"Order must be restored,
the Freedman's Bureau a sword at our throat,
our old life stolen,
how else to fight?"

And yet,
there is another voice,
quiet but seething,
that murmurs from the same page,
"This Klan…this ghost of war,
is not the resurrection of the South,
but the devil himself, come up from the earth,
feeding on our blood."

Knights of the Ku Klux Klan, they call themselves,
and in their hoods, their robes,
they claim a birthright,

a right to lash the darkness back into chains.
Pulaski trembles, Memphis waits.

But when did it become justice
to ride through fields with fire?
When did it become necessary
to make a man less than a man,
his skin a crime?

The year 1866, the Appeal declares,
a time of peace that feels like war.
Families torn apart once more,
not by cannon fire, but by fear.
A new rebellion,
this one born in silence,
marches forward.

The 13th Amendment: Voices in the Moment

In the halls of Congress,
echoes of chains still rattle,
though the ink dries on the parchment.
1865, and the law has been written:
"No more slavery," it says,
but the air is thick with unsaid words.

A Northern Congressman speaks:
"We've torn the root from the soil,
uprooted this sin,
declared men as men,
not as property.
Let it be known,
this is the first real victory,
this is America, reborn."
He sits, hands trembling,
as if the ghosts of the past
are pressing upon him still.

A Southern voice rises, bitter:
"What will you give me now,
for the cotton that no longer bleeds?
What will you say to the soil
that can no longer be tilled
by those we bought and owned?"
He looks down the long road home,
sees the fields empty, the hands idle.
"They call it freedom,
but what will come of us now,
when the land is no longer ours to command?"

A freed man listens in the distance, his voice quiet, uncertain:
"I woke today to a different sun,
one not shadowed by the master's whip.
But still, I tremble.
For what is freedom
when you have no home, no land,
when the world does not yet know your name?
I am unchained, yes,
but the road ahead is long,
and my feet are tired already."

A mother, born in chains, whispers to her children:
"We will not forget what they took from us,
but look—today the chains are broken.
We are not what we were yesterday.
We walk free now, into a new world.
But oh, child, freedom is not easy.
It comes with shadows of its own."

A Northern abolitionist cries out:
"This is the day we dreamed of,
fought for, prayed for.
But it is not the end—
no, it is only a crack in the wall.
What of their rights?
What of their voices?
There are still battles to be won."
She knows that paper cannot hold
the weight of a nation's guilt,
that the ink is only the start.

And still, the South whispers back:
"This is the devil's doing.
You cannot erase what has always been.
You cannot strip the chains from the past
without breaking something in us all."
They close their doors,
but they cannot shut out the wind of change.

The 13th Amendment is signed,
but the nation is not healed.
Voices still rise, from the fields,
from the broken homes,
from the hearts of those freed
and those left behind.
Freedom, they know, is never just a word—
it is a fight,
a promise yet to be kept.

The Freedmen's Bureau. 1865

They came with books
and bandages,
with promises woven in paper
and hands outstretched.
A bureau of hope, they called it,
carving a path for the newly freed
to walk on their own.

In the dim light of makeshift classrooms,
letters unfolded—
A, B, C—
the first taste of a future
not written by others.

Doctors tended wounds
still raw from chains,
while fields lay silent,
the cotton now untouched,
the soil restless under new feet.

But outside the walls,
the South still clenched its teeth,
whispers of rebellion curling in the wind.
"This is not how it's meant to be,"
they said, eyes hard,
hands clutching a past they couldn't release.

The Bureau, noble as its mission,
faced a tide of hate—
schools burned, contracts torn,
freedom tangled in the ropes of old fear.

And yet,
still they came,
still they taught,
still they healed,
holding the fragile line
between what was,
and what might be.

Andrew Johnson's Reconstruction, 1865-1867

He stood,
firm in his belief,
that the South should rise again
with old scars unbandaged.
No punishment, no reckoning—
just a hand extended
to those who turned their backs
on the Union once.

Leniency, he called it,
as he vetoed the bills
that might have stitched the nation
back together—
civil rights denied,
justice paused,
freedom still hanging
by a fraying thread.

In the halls of Congress,
voices rose like storms,
thunder clashing against his will.
The Radical Republicans, fists clenched,
saw his betrayal of the freed,
of the Union loyalists who bled
to break the chains.

And those chains—
not yet rusted away—
still clung to the ankles
of the newly freed,
their hopes tied to laws
that never came.
Promises whispered in the wind,
but Johnson's pen struck them down.

A South rebuilt,
but in shadows,
with the same old hands
holding the reins.
His policies,
soft as the soil turned by the plow,
let the past root itself

deeper into the land.

And so,
freedom waited,
silent,
as the vetoes stacked,
while the nation's soul frayed
beneath the weight of his easy hand.

The Memphis Riots, 1866

The smoke rose high above the street,
where peace had barely found its way.
The cries of hate and anger beat,
on souls who'd just seen freedom's day.

The Black men stood, their heads held tall,
Union soldiers who fought for the land.
But the white mob gathered, seeking to maul,
with torches and rage in every hand.

Homes were burned, the night turned red,
while mothers clutched their children tight.
In Memphis, hope and fear were wed,
in shadows cast by hate's cruel light.

The veterans fought, though tired from war,
their battlefields had shifted home.
But even here, on freedom's shore,
they found no refuge from the storm.

The fragile peace, so newly born,
was shattered by the mob's harsh hand.
The city's heart, once torn by war,
bled again across the land.

And in the morning, ashes lay,
where lives and dreams had once stood strong.
The Memphis sun rose cold that day,
as justice wept for all gone wrong.

The Colfax Massacre, 1873

They stood at the courthouse,
a line drawn in the dust,
the weight of freedom resting on tired shoulders,
guns held not for power,
but for survival.
Black men—militia, defenders—
their eyes fixed on the promise
that had come too late
and too fragile.

In Colfax, the air was thick
with the heat of old hate,
a South that refused to let go
of what was stolen,
what was broken,
clinging still to chains unseen.

The white mob came,
faces hard as iron,
marching with the memory of a past
they couldn't bear to lose.
They called it justice,
as they raised their rifles,
as they laid siege
to the courthouse,
a fortress of hope
made from bricks too weak to stand.

For hours they fought,
Black men pressing back the tide,
knowing the cost,
feeling the breath of death
on their necks.
But no cavalry came,
no government hand
reached down to pull them from the fire.

And then, it was over—
not in surrender,
but in blood.
Over 100 lives taken,
names lost to the wind,

bodies left in the earth
that could no longer hold the weight
of their struggle.
The courthouse fell silent,
a tomb for dreams buried in violence,
and the nation turned away,
blind to the massacre
written in Colfax soil.

Federal protection,
just words on a page,
gone with the smoke that rose
into a sky that had seen too much.
Colfax became another wound,
another scar,
on the body of a country
still learning what freedom truly costs.

Jim Crow Laws

A line drawn,
not in sand,
but in skin,
etched in the cracks
of sidewalks and storefronts,
whispered in the hush
of courtroom gavel,
carved in church pews
where prayer was blind.

Water fountains—
separate streams,
but the same thirst.

A veil draped over justice,
where "freedom"
was spelled in white letters,
while Black bodies
bent beneath the weight
of silent chains.

Jim Crow—
not a man,
but a shadow,
longer than any whip,
darker than any night.

The North After the War

The factories hum again,
not for cannon or bullet,
but for the work of hands rebuilding.
In the cool mornings,
men rise with the sun,
sleeves rolled up,
not for war,
but for the rhythm of the forge,
the grain of wood,
the shaping of iron into plowshares.

There's a quiet hope
on these streets,
where once soldiers marched home—
now, children play,
their laughter threading through the alleys
like a promise kept.

Neighbors talk again,
voices softer,
the burden of loss shared
over coffee in the early light.
Men with lined faces,
scarred but standing,
build new cities with the bones of the old.
Together they rebuild what was broken,
not by brick alone,
but with the slow weaving
of trust,
of hands held out to one another.

The North, scarred,
but mending,
heals not in grand gestures,
but in the daily labor
of living
and moving forward.

The South After the War

The land breathes,
quiet now,
fields once scarred by battle
find life again in the hands of men,
once divided,
now sowing seeds
not of war, but of harvest.

The South remembers,
but it does not linger.
The soil still knows the weight of footsteps,
but today,
it knows the hands of all men,
freed,
and finding their way
through the same earth.

In the slow mornings,
families gather under broad oak trees,
sharing stories of old
while the future hums in the air.
The cotton fields sway,
but no longer in silence.
Voices rise—not in anger,
but in song,
work songs turned to hymns
for a new day.

Neighbors, once at odds,
speak now of rebuilding,
not in grand speeches,
but in the shared labor of the farm,
of children born into a world
where the past lingers,
but no longer binds.

The South,
learning to heal,
one field, one family,
one conversation at a time,
grows again
in ways war could never touch.

1890s America

In the North, the forges blaze and burn,
Wheels of progress twist and turn.
Cities climb where rivers wind,
A land of change, with work in mind.

Trains whistle through the crowded streets,
Progress strides with iron feet.
Workers toil from dawn till night,
Chasing dreams in electric light.

But in the South, the fields still sway,
Cotton blooms in the heat of day.
The soil, once torn by war and pain,
Now feels the plow, but bears the stain.

Voices rise in gospel song,
Hoping to right what's long been wrong.
Hands that built on broken ground,
Now seek a future, still unbound.

From North to South, the times collide,
Two different paths, one nation's pride.
The 1890s, full of strife,
A country searching for its life.

Next Up: Chapter 6: 20th Century America (1900-1999): The 20th century arrived like a thunderclap, shaking the world awake with the roar of industry and the hum of electrified cities. It heralded an era of boundless ambition, where steel and steam redefined the skyline and human aspirations soared to the skies and beyond. Yet beneath the gleam of progress lay deepening shadows, as new inventions brought both promise and peril, forever altering the course of history.

Chapter 6: 20th Century America (1900-1999)

The U.S. Civil War's legacy extended into the 20th century, not through fighting on a battlefield, but through seismic societal, political, and cultural shifts that redefined the nation. The rapid acceleration of immigration, urbanization, and industrialization in the early 1900s forever altered the American landscape. Cities swelled as immigrants poured in from Europe, and African Americans began migrating from the rural South during the Great Migration, searching for industrial jobs in the North. While they escaped the oppressive Jim Crow laws, they were met with new forms of systemic discrimination in housing, education, and employment, especially in urban centers. This period of transformation intertwined with the industrial might built during World War I and World War II, wars that propelled the U.S. into global dominance. Yet, the wars exposed a national hypocrisy—how could America fight for freedom abroad while maintaining racial inequality at home?

The echoes of the Civil War resonated deeply in the civil rights movement of the 1950s and 1960s, a modern battle to realize the freedoms promised but never fully delivered. African Americans, joined by women and other marginalized groups, pressed for full citizenship through voting rights, equal protection under the law, and freedom from racial violence. Their persistent efforts led to monumental victories such as the Voting Rights Act and Civil Rights Act, but deep-rooted inequalities persisted.

As the 20th century advanced, the transformations of globalization and deindustrialization compounded the challenges. Once-thriving industrial towns, particularly in the Rust Belt, became hollowed out by outsourcing, leading to economic despair, disillusionment, and political volatility. The division widened further during the Vietnam War, with anti-war protests revealing deep fissures in society and disillusionment with government, much like the earlier conflicts that had marked the nation's history.

The political landscape swung dramatically between liberal movements, such as those championed by the women's liberation movement and the 1973

Roe v. Wade decision, and conservative reactions aimed at curbing the advancements of civil rights and economic equality. The Watergate scandal and rampant corporate greed revealed during this time eroded public trust in both government and big business, exposing the darker side of American capitalism. Corruption, racial tensions, and class inequalities were all magnified under the pressures of modernity.

By the close of the 20th century, many of the ideological battles from the Civil War—over the definition of freedom, equality, and what it truly means to be an American—were still being fought. These battles had evolved and taken new forms but remained refracted through the complexities of modernity. The economic inequalities and social tensions that emerged in the post-Civil War period had not dissipated but deepened, shaping the country into the contentious, divided landscape we continue to grapple with today.

Lingering Cleavages of Black and White

The line is still there,
etched deep, unseen but felt,
running through streets, schools, churches—
neighborhoods split by skin,
hearts divided by history.

The war ended,
the chains were broken,
but the cleavages never healed.
They linger in whispers,
in looks, in unspoken rules—
what side you should live on,
where you're not welcome.

Black and white,
two colors bound by the same nation,
still separated by the scars
of what once was
and what still is.

Resentment about Southern European Immigration

They came,
dark-haired, olive-skinned,
speaking tongues that sounded strange,
eyes full of hope,
hands ready for work,
but the gates weren't open wide.

"Too many," they said,
"Too different, too loud, too bold."
The land of liberty had its limits,
its walls hidden beneath the stars and stripes.

In the factories, in the streets,
resentment grew,
against the new,
against the unfamiliar faces
from Italy, Greece, and Spain,
who brought their food, their faith,
but found the welcome thin.

The Second Rise of the Klan, 1915

They rose again,
from the ashes of hate,
hoods pulled tight against the world,
crosses burned into the night.

Not just the South this time,
but everywhere they could spread—
their message draped in patriotism,
their fear masked as pride.

Against Black, against Jew,
against anyone who didn't fit
their twisted dream of purity.
The Klan marched again,
a shadow over the land,
while the world watched,
silent.

What World War I Meant to Americans, Black and White

The war was over there,
but its ripples came home.
White and Black fought,
side by side,
in the trenches, in the mud.

But when they returned,
the lines were drawn again.
Victory tasted different—
for some, a hero's welcome;
for others, a reminder
that not even war could change
what color meant.

For Black men,
who had worn the uniform,
there were no parades.
The country they defended
still refused to defend them.

The Roaring Twenties That Roared for Some, But Not Many

It was jazz,
champagne bubbles bursting,
flappers dancing under electric lights.
It was stock markets soaring,
men in suits, women in pearls,
living high on the promise
that the good times would never end.

But outside the cities,
the fields were dry,
the factories still clanked with labor,
the roar was a whisper
for those who toiled,
for those whose pockets
were already empty.

The 20s roared for the few,
while the many
waited for a turn
that never came.

The Great Depression: Rich and Poor, Black and White

When it hit,
it hit everyone.
The rich fell from their towers of wealth,
the poor sank deeper into the earth.
White faces lined up in soup kitchens,
but Black faces, already hungry,
stood behind them.

The banks closed,
the dust rose,
and in the South,
sharecroppers, Black and white,
scratched at the land,
hoping for something,
anything,
to grow.

The Depression had no favorites,
but its bite left marks
on those who were already
struggling to stand.

World War II, Hitler, and the Jews

In towns under skies stained with smoke,
the streets turn hollow,
footsteps replaced by whispers of the disappeared.
Windows, once warm with candlelight,
now empty as glass-eyed ghosts.
Children vanish into the dusk,
clutched by the cold hands of soldiers,
who speak in commands, their words
like boots crushing soft earth.

In the small cities,
Reich banners blacken the horizon,
the Führer's shadow crawls over Europe,
its grip tightening—
crushing life with the precision of jackboots.
Laughter and light shatter under the weight of hate,
children dragged from doorways,
their faces pressed to cold walls,
as the Gestapo's breath lingers, thick as death in the air.

In Auschwitz, Buchenwald, Dachau,
the gates yawn open,
a steel mouth swallowing all that enters.
"Arbeit Macht Frei" screams from above,
a mocking whisper from Himmler's lips,
while Mengele's cold hands—
scalpels of horror—
cut into souls already bleeding.
The air, thick with silence
where screams once hung like fog.
Flesh, once whole and warm,
burns in the belly of the beast,
leaving only ash—
a snow that falls too slowly
over the fields of barbed wire.

Goebbels' lies fill the air like poison,
turning neighbors into enemies.
The stars on the windows, yellow and bright,
become targets for Kristallnacht's fury,
shards of glass cutting the night like screams
that never find an end.

Old women sit by crumbled hearths,
knitting the names of lost sons
into the threads of their grief.
The trains howl through the night,
each whistle a funeral dirge,
souls packed tighter than air—
heads shaved, eyes buried
in places they have yet to see.

The SS, in their cold steel armor,
load the trains with faces lost to the void.
Hitler's eyes burn with conquest,
his venomous voice echoing through Warsaw's empty streets,
through Treblinka's cries.
And in the end, when the war's roar fades,
the bones of millions lie beneath silent ground,
rising as dust in the wind,
carved into the history of Europe.
A scar too deep to heal.

Only the ghosts remain—
rising in the breath of chimneys,
etched in the walls of empty homes,
carved into the silence of a Europe
rebuilt upon bone and ash.

Red Scare and McCarthyism

Fear spread like wildfire,
unchecked, unchallenged,
a nation gripped by the ghosts of enemies unseen.
Communism—
a word that made neighbors suspicious,
made friendships fragile.

McCarthy rose,
with his lists and accusations,
a man with power to destroy
by faint murmur.
Actors, teachers, workers—
all could fall,
all could burn
under the heat of fear.

The Red Scare left scars,
not in battlefields,
but in living rooms,
where trust had been shattered.

The Beat Generation

In smoky cafes, under the dim hum of neon,
they whispered revolution,
voices rising like jazz notes,
sharp and syncopated, breaking free,
dancing through the haze of cigarette clouds—
their words wild, untamed,
and full of fire.

On the road, with nothing
but a beat-up Chevy and a soul burning for freedom,
Kerouac carved the map of a new America,
a landscape of highways and endless sky,
where hitchhikers and poets roamed,
where rest stops became sacred temples
to the wanderlust of lost souls.
He pressed his words like ink onto the asphalt,
each tire spin a new line of prose—
spontaneous, alive,
chasing meaning in the spaces between miles.

And Ginsberg,
howling at the moon of America's despair,
stood on the rooftops of the disillusioned,
his voice echoing through the canyons of Wall Street,
"Capitalism is killing us!" he screamed.
"Machines are devouring the human soul!"
His words tore through the air like a tempest,
unafraid of the taboos,
the dark corners where society tried to hide
its madness and its lust,
its broken promises of freedom.

They sought more than suburban lawns,
more than 9-to-5 drudgery and white picket fences—
the Beats wanted truth,
raw and ragged,
felt through the pulse of their blood,
in the ecstasy of a jazz solo,
the deep hum of a Buddhist chant,
or the swirling colors of an acid trip.
And they found it,
in the smoky rooms of San Francisco,

in New York alleyways,
on the roads that stretched beyond the horizon.

Burroughs cut his sentences like a blade,
slicing through the veils of reality,
exposing the rot at the heart of America's dream.
In Naked Lunch, he laid it bare,
a country addicted to control,
to power, to the needle in its vein,
and he asked us—how do we escape this machine?

In search of meaning, they turned east—
to Zen, to Dharma, to meditation.
The Beats craved something real,
something that couldn't be bought
or sold or packaged.
They found solace in silence,
in the simple breath that reminded them
they were still alive,
still fighting against the tidal wave of conformity
that threatened to swallow them whole.

They scrawled poems on napkins,
on gas station receipts,
on the backs of diner menus,
anywhere they could capture the fleeting thoughts
that blazed through their minds like fireflies.
There were no rules, no forms to follow—
only the rhythm of life,
the beat of the universe
that pulsed through their veins.

And in the end, their words became a movement,
a spark that lit the fires of the 1960s,
fueling the dreams of a generation
that refused to be chained
by the weight of expectations.
The Beat Generation carved their names
into the heart of America,
forever etched into the highways
where wanderers still roam,
looking for meaning
in the chaos of a world gone mad.

The Civil Rights Movement

It wasn't just marches,
it was a tide—
slow at first, then rising,
until it swept through cities and streets,
through hearts that had been closed.

Selma, Birmingham, Washington—
names that became symbols
of a fight too long delayed.

Black men and women,
young and old,
walked with courage
against hoses, dogs, and bullets,
demanding what had always been theirs—
equality,
freedom,
dignity.

Reverend Martin Luther King's Life and Legacy

It began, as all things do,
with a boy, born into the world,
not knowing yet the weight
he would carry.
Atlanta was his home,
a place where skin spoke before words did,
where the lines were drawn
not in sand,
but in stone.

Martin, they called him—
a name that would echo
through streets and hearts,
but back then, he was just a boy,
running through the halls of Ebenezer Baptist,
his father's church.
He learned early about faith,
how it could lift you up
even when the world tried to push you down.

His voice was strong,
even then,
and he carried that voice
through school,
through college,
until it became more than just sound.
It became a call—
a call to something bigger,
a call to justice,
a call to the dream
that lived inside him.

He found his way to Montgomery,
a city heavy with history,
with the weight of what it meant to be Black
in the South.
Rosa had sat,
refusing to move,
and Martin, now a reverend,
stood up.

He didn't carry a weapon.

No, his weapon was words—
words sharper than any blade,
softer than any whisper,
but powerful enough
to bring a nation to its knees.

They marched,
through the streets of Montgomery,
and the streets of Selma,
and everywhere in between.
They marched for the right to sit,
to vote,
to be.
And with every step,
his voice grew louder,
until the whole world
could hear it.

But it wasn't easy.
It never is,
when you're speaking truth
to a world built on lies.
They threatened him,
called him names,
threw him in jail,
tried to break him—
but they couldn't.

He stood in Washington,
in front of the Lincoln Memorial,
and the world stood with him.
Hundreds of thousands of faces,
Black and white,
looking up at a man
who carried the weight of their hopes
on his shoulders.

"I have a dream," he said.
Four words that would echo
long after his voice went silent.
A dream of a world
where his children,
our children,

would not be judged
by the color of their skin
but by the content of their character.

It was a dream,
but it was also a promise.
A promise that one day,
we would see each other
for what we are—
not as enemies,
not as strangers,
but as brothers,
as sisters,
as one people.

But the world wasn't ready
for that kind of promise.
And so they tried to stop him.
In 1968, in Memphis,
they took his life—
shot him down
on the balcony of a motel,
as if a bullet could silence a man
whose voice had already risen
above the clouds.

But they were wrong.
They couldn't stop him.
Because even in death,
his legacy lived on—
in the marches that followed,
in the laws that changed,
in the hearts of the people
who carried his dream forward.

We remember him now,
not just as a man,
but as a movement.
A movement that keeps marching,
even when the road is long,
even when the world pushes back.

His life was a beacon,

a light in the darkness,
showing us the way
toward justice,
toward peace,
toward a future
where all are free.

And his legacy?
It's in every step we take
toward that dream,
every word we speak
for justice,
for equality,
for love.

Reverend Martin Luther King,
gone from this world,
but never truly gone.
Because his dream lives on,
in each of us,
as we march
toward a better tomorrow.

The Sound of Change

The strum of the guitar, raw and wild,
echoes through the streets, the smoky clubs,
where Dylan's voice—ragged and sharp as wind through autumn leaves—
speaks of a world that needs to break free.
"The times, they are a-changin'," he sang,
his words a banner for the restless and the hopeful,
the seekers and the outcasts,
calling out to the streets where protest chants rise
like smoke from cities on fire.

Joan Baez stands beside him,
her voice like a river cutting through stone,
singing of peace, justice, and a dream
where no one is silenced, where freedom rings
from Selma to Washington.
Her songs rise above the sirens,
above the fear,
and flow into the hearts of the weary and the brave,
calling for hands to join,
for a march toward something better.

Their music, a lifeline in a world split wide open—
it drifts from open windows,
from radios in greasy diners,
and whispers to those who know
that change isn't coming—it's already here.
Through notes of rock 'n' roll, rebellion blooms,
as guitars scream for freedom,
their feedback buzzing with discontent.

Woodstock's muddy fields felt the pulse,
as Hendrix's electric fingers rewrote the anthem,
stretching "The Star-Spangled Banner"
into a cry for a country that was losing its way.
Janis Joplin's voice cracked and soared,
a wild flame burning through the night,
while Richie Havens sang freedom with hands calloused from the struggle.

Folk and rock intertwined,
a protest hymn played with distortion and soul,
where Lennon's peace and love melted into Dylan's hard truths.
The stage became a battlefield,

where songs fought against war, racism, injustice,
where harmonicas and tambourines
became weapons for those without a voice.

And the message still rings—
echoes in the air like an unresolved chord,
as voices rise again,
calling out from protests in the streets,
marching to the beat of change,
the songs still ringing in our ears.

Voices of Black Writers and Poets in the 20th Century

Langston Hughes, Zora Neale Hurston, James Baldwin,
voices that carried the weight
of history and hope.
Their words weren't just ink
on paper,
they were bridges—
spanning the chasm
between what America was
and what it could be.

Poems, stories,
born of struggle,
but full of beauty,
songs of survival,
and dreams deferred
but not forgotten.

They wrote for the world,
but spoke for the soul
of Black America.

Vietnam: Black and White Soldiers

In the jungle,
there was no Black, no white—
just green uniforms,
boots sinking in the same mud.
They fought together,
bled together,
died together.

But when the war was over,
they came home
to different worlds.
White soldiers found parades,
or at least understanding.
Black soldiers returned to the same fight
they'd left behind—
a country still at war
with itself.

In Vietnam,
they were brothers.
Back home,
they were strangers again.

The Fall of the Berlin Wall, 1989

A wall,
built from fear,
brick by brick,
to keep two worlds apart.

But walls cannot hold forever.
In 1989,
it crumbled—
not with a crash,
but with hands tearing at the stones,
voices shouting freedom
on both sides.

East met West,
and the Cold War ended,
not with missiles,
but with hope,
as families reunited,
and the world exhaled.

Fire in the Streets

The streets smolder in the heat of summer,
burning not with sunlight, but with rage—
Watts, Hough, Newark, Detroit—
the names spill like smoke
from broken windows and burned-out storefronts,
from neighborhoods where promises never came
and hope feels like a stranger.

In Watts, it begins with a single spark—
a traffic stop under the weight of August skies,
and then the streets explode,
like a volcano long dormant.
The people rise, fists clenched,
voices cracking through the din of sirens.
For six long days, the sky above Los Angeles
is thick with fire,
smoke curling like angry ghosts
from buildings left as skeletons.

And in Cleveland's Hough,
the summer of '66 comes heavy with fear.
The rumors, the whispers of violence,
spark like a match,
and soon the streets bleed red,
bottles of gasoline, fists of fury,
rage against the walls of a city that forgot its own.
Windows shattered, dreams slipping through the cracks,
and on the corner, children watch
as their world burns—
the flames a reflection in their wide, silent eyes.

Detroit is a drumbeat in '67,
louder than the Motown tunes once sung
on these same streets.
The tanks roll in,
the soldiers in their helmets,
but they can't stop the fires,
they can't quiet the roar
of a city that has been pushed too far.
Black bodies, bent beneath the weight of injustice,
rise in the glow of the flames,
and the night screams with the sound of shattering glass.

The National Guard is called,
but the soldiers are not saviors.
They are a wall, a threat,
a reminder of the distance between two Americas—
one of power, one of struggle.

In Newark, the streets pulse with fury,
another traffic stop, another spark.
And now, five days of flames,
five days of anger uncoiled from decades of neglect.
The smoke doesn't ask questions,
it rises, silent and bitter,
curling through alleys and over rooftops,
as if to claim the city itself.

Across urban America, the cities burn—
a message scrawled in the language of fire and glass.
Watts, Cleveland, Newark, Detroit,
each one a cry,
a scream that reverberates
through the country's concrete veins.
No justice, no peace—
the refrain echoes,
an anthem of the streets,
where the flames tell a story
that no one wanted to hear.

But beneath the riot, beneath the ash and debris,
there is more—
there are lives, beaten down, ignored,
pushed to the edge where there is no choice
but to fight, to claw, to scream.
And in the wake of the destruction,
as the fires cool and the smoke clears,
the questions remain,
smoldering in the hearts of those left behind.

What does it mean to rise?
What does it take to be heard?
And how long can a city burn
before it burns itself out?

What the 20th Century Did and Did Not Learn

The Civil War,
they said,
was the great reckoning,
a fight to tear the roots of hatred
from the soil of a nation,
to pull them out,
bloody and twisted,
and lay them bare
for all to see.

We learned, or so they thought,
that freedom cannot be chained,
that people are not property,
that a man's worth
is not the color of his skin.

But the 20th century came
and the lessons bled through
the cracks of time,
fading like old ink
on fragile paper.

We built monuments to the war,
stone soldiers standing tall,
but forgot what they stood for,
forgot that the end of slavery
was not the end of the fight.

Jim Crow rose like a specter,
a shadow cast over the South,
whispering that the war may be over,
but the battle never was.
Separate but equal,
they said,
but the weight of it all
was never equal,
and the chains that fell away
were replaced by walls
in schools, in neighborhoods,
in the silence of white faces
turned away.

The 20th century remembered
the battles fought with guns,
with brothers at arms,
but forgot the war within—
the one that raged in hearts,
the one that wasn't won
by surrender
but by love,
by justice,
by seeing what was once
refused to be seen.

We marched again,
a century later,
through the same streets,
Selma, Montgomery—
names that should've been left
in history's books
but had to be spoken
once more.
The dream deferred,
the promise broken,
the war's roots still tangled
in the nation's soul.

What did we learn?
That laws can be passed,
but hearts take longer to heal.
That freedom isn't just a declaration,
it's a practice,
a daily struggle
to pull those roots up,
again and again,
until nothing is left
but the soil
where new things can grow.

The 20th century built bridges,
yes,
but too many stood over rivers
still filled with blood.
We learned how to fight,
but not always how to make peace.

We learned the cost of division,
but still paid the price
again and again.

What the war left us,
we carried into the century,
but the lesson—the true lesson—
is still being learned.

Motown

Motown, born from Detroit's heartbeat,
a city of industry, where machines roared
and dreams danced in the streets.
It wasn't just music—it was a movement,
a rhythm of change, a soulful cry
for something more.

Berry Gordy saw it first,
the pulse in the people,
the way songs could mend
what the world tried to break.
He built a sound, polished it smooth,
and let it glide like a Cadillac
down endless roads of possibility.

Stevie Wonder,
his fingers flying across keys,
spoke of inner visions
we couldn't yet see.
And Smokey Robinson,
his voice a whisper, a fire,
singing "Tracks of My Tears,"
and we all felt the hurt,
the yearning.

Diana Ross and the Supremes—
"Stop! In the Name of Love"—
they gave the heartbreak a beat,
made it something you could dance to.
The Temptations made it real,
"Papa Was a Rolling Stone,"
and Marvin Gaye asked us all,
"What's Going On?"—
his voice a plea for justice,
for peace, for love in the chaos.

Motown was born in the shadows
of segregation, in a world
divided by color and hate.
But the music brought us together,
lifting voices above the noise,
above the pain.

Love and heartbreak, struggle and joy—
they were the themes,
woven into every note,
every rhythm.

It was music that could not be silenced,
not by borders, not by fear.
It crossed lines, reached into homes
and hearts, brought people
to their feet and to each other.
Motown, the sound of soul,
of a people's perseverance,
became America's song,
the world's echo.

Today, it still breathes,
in the grooves of vinyl,
in the chorus of memories,
because love, hope, and freedom—
those things never die.
Motown didn't just make music.
It made a legacy,
and we're still swaying
to its rhythm.

Next Up: Chapter 7: 21st Century America (2000-Present): The 21st century dawned in a blaze of digital light, connecting the world in an instant and forever changing how we live, work, and communicate. It ushered in an age of unprecedented innovation, where technology blurred the lines between the physical and virtual, reshaping societies at breakneck speed. Yet, amid the promises of progress, it brought stark reminders of global challenges—climate change, inequality, and shifting geopolitics—demanding a new kind of resilience and vision for the future.

Chapter 7: 21st Century America (2000-Present)

In the 21st century, the unresolved conflicts of the U.S. Civil War reemerged in new and complex forms, shaped by technological advances, political upheavals, and cultural revolutions. The rise of the digital economy and the internet reshaped labor and social interactions, creating unprecedented global connectivity while simultaneously deepening economic divides. Many Americans found themselves trapped in cycles of precarious employment and gig work, with automation and the outsourcing of jobs leading to the disappearance of traditional manufacturing roles, particularly in regions like the Rust Belt. This sense of economic dislocation echoed the tensions from the 19th century, where shifts in labor and economy sowed discord and division.

The 9/11 attacks in 2001 marked a seismic shift in national identity, leading to protracted wars in Afghanistan and Iraq that reignited public debates over freedom, democracy, and the role of the U.S. on the world stage. Like Vietnam, these wars fostered deep disillusionment with government motives and accountability, fueling growing skepticism about U.S. leadership abroad. As the century progressed, immigration once again became a political flashpoint, with polarizing debates about borders, national identity, and who is entitled to the American Dream. These discussions became intertwined with broader cultural questions about inclusion, as economic inequality continued to widen and globalization primarily benefited corporations and the wealthy elite, leaving large swaths of the population facing stagnant wages and diminishing job security.

Political polarization intensified, with sharp swings between Republican and Democratic leadership. The election of Barack Obama in 2008 was seen as a symbol of racial progress but also provoked an intense backlash from conservative movements. Black Lives Matter and #MeToo emerged as powerful grassroots movements highlighting the ongoing struggles against racial and gender inequalities, while voter suppression efforts and gerrymandering echoed the disenfranchisement tactics of the past, particularly during the Reconstruction and Jim Crow eras.

In 2016, the election of Donald Trump marked a shift toward populism and nationalism, emphasizing the deep divide between rural and urban America, much like the regional tensions that fueled the Civil War. The rhetoric of "America First" and a focus on isolationism, border control, and trade protectionism further highlighted these divides. Political debates grew more extreme, with the polarization of media, rise of dark money in elections, and scandals like those following the 2008 financial crisis and corporate corruption amplifying the public's mistrust of institutions.

Beyond domestic issues, global crises such as climate change and pandemics like COVID-19 heightened a pervasive sense of instability and unease. As technology advanced at a dizzying pace, with the rise of artificial intelligence, surveillance capitalism, and social media monopolies, Americans grappled with the very nature of work, identity, and privacy in the digital age.

Much like the Civil War era, the defining question of the 21st century remains centered on identity: Who belongs in America? As the United States continues to grow more diverse through immigration and evolving cultural dynamics, the question of national identity has only become more pressing. From debates about citizenship, immigrant rights, and the treatment of refugees to discussions about what it means to be "American" in a country with increasingly pluralistic values, the question of belonging touches every facet of public discourse. Political movements and national debates over issues like DACA (Deferred Action for Childhood Arrivals) and family separations at the border have sparked national conversations about the nation's moral and ethical responsibilities toward those seeking a place in the country.

What does it mean to be a citizen in a nation grappling with pluralism, economic disparity, and the promises of democracy? Citizenship in the United States is no longer solely about legal status; it has become a broader cultural question about inclusion, rights, and representation. The struggle for racial justice, as seen through movements like Black Lives Matter, and ongoing challenges to voter rights echo the post-Civil War Reconstruction era when newly freed African Americans fought for equal citizenship under the law. Today, marginalized communities continue to face systemic obstacles, and the debate around voting rights, policing, economic opportunities, and access to healthcare is deeply intertwined with the larger question of what citizenship—and its privileges—should entail in a modern democracy. The gulf between wealth and poverty, too, has widened dramatically, testing the American ideal of equal opportunity and upward mobility.

As the century unfolds, the battles over freedom, equality, and justice are increasingly refracted through the complexities of modern life, with technology adding a new layer of tension to these age-old struggles. The rapid pace of technological innovation has both democratized information and intensified political divides, with social media amplifying extremes and misinformation spreading rapidly. The rise of surveillance technologies, the digital economy, and artificial intelligence poses new questions about rights and freedoms, from privacy to job security. Yet, the echoes of the past remain unmistakably present as many of these struggles are rooted in foundational conflicts over who holds power, whose voices matter, and what kind of society America will become. The Civil War may have ended over 160 years ago, but the nation's ongoing fights over identity, citizenship, and democracy reflect its lingering influence. Ultimately, the vision of America that prevails in the 21st century will shape not only its own future but will have profound implications for the rest of the world.

Gerrymandered Ohio

In the crooked corners of Ohio,
where the land stretches in forgotten folds,
they carve lines not with care,
but with the sharp edge of power,
dividing valleys and rivers for their convenience.
The landscape—Hocking Hills, the Maumee River,
and Cleveland's industrial sprawl—
bends to their will, like a map reshaped by unseen hands.

Here, where cornfields roll into suburbs,
they draw the lines, precise and surgical,
not for the people, but for the pocketbooks
of those who count their power in votes,
their wealth in policies passed
while Main Street watches, silent and splintered.
It's a war without guns,
fought on paper,
with numbers twisted to favor
the few who laugh behind closed doors.

Districts snake through neighborhoods like rivers of ink,
twisting, turning, cutting across places
where one town's voice meets another's silence.
From Cincinnati to Youngstown,
they carve out kingdoms,
invisible to the naked eye but felt in every vote,
a place where democracy cracks
beneath the weight of the lines drawn
for convenience, not for justice.

In Toledo, the borders shift like whispers in the dark,
cutting through streets and schools,
leaving voters at the mercy of demagogues
who speak not for the people,
but for the highest bidder,
filling their coffers with promises and power.

And yet the battle rages,
a fight not between swords but ballots,
where the right pulls tight on one side,
the left clenches fists on the other,
and those in between—

the factory workers, the farmers, the teachers—
are left wondering where their voices went.

This is gerrymandered Ohio,
where the future is shaped
not by the people's hands,
but by those who twist the lines to fit their gain,
leaving behind landscapes of frustration
and fields of forgotten dreams.

There must be a better way—
to draw lines that let the people breathe,
to carve paths where every voice matters,
where democracy stands on solid ground,
not splintered by the weight of greed,
but lifted by the hands of those
who believe in something more.

Sadly, Ohio Issue 1,
aimed at drawing more equitable lines,
failed at the hands of Ohio voters,
leaving us with boundaries,
impeding voices meant to unite.

People of All Colors and Persuasions

We are a mosaic,
each tile unique, each shade different,
yet when we come together,
we make a whole.
From the streets of Harlem
to the fields of California,
we are a country that hums
with the voices of many.

African Americans, whose history
is etched in the soil, in the hands
that built this nation,
still rising, still pushing forward,
carrying the weight of generations
but refusing to be crushed.

Hispanics, with rhythms in their veins,
their cultures weaving together
language and laughter,
family and faith,
bringing the warmth of a thousand suns
into cold corners,
reminding us all of resilience.

Asians, with roots in the East
but dreams planted here,
balancing tradition and the new,
shaping cities, shaping minds,
a quiet strength that flows
like rivers through the heart of this land.

And Whites, too,
part of this tapestry,
carving out their stories
from mountains and prairies,
from privilege and hardship,
learning what it means
to share space in a world
they once believed was only theirs.

We are men, women,
and everything in between,

young and old,
some who move fast,
some who take their time.
The LGBTQ+ community,
standing tall in their truth,
no longer hidden in shadows,
but shining like bright stars
that refuse to be dimmed.

We are different, yes—
but not divided.
Not truly.
We live in the same air,
breathe the same hopes,
feel the same fears.
Yet, there are those who long
for simpler days,
a black-and-white America
where lines were drawn
and never crossed.
They speak of the past
as if it were a golden age,
but forget the chains,
the silence, the walls
that kept so many out.

We know better now.
We must do better.
For balance is not found
in sameness,
but in the dance between
what makes us different
and what makes us the same.

We need to let go
of what we think we know—
the boxes, the labels,
the maps drawn by old hands
that never saw the whole picture.
We must build a new world,
where the colors mix freely,
where persuasions don't divide us
but enrich us.

We are all in it together,
no matter where we come from,
what we look like,
who we love,
what we call ourselves.
America is not a fixed thing,
not a relic of the past,
but a living, breathing dream
that belongs to everyone.

Let us hold each other up,
not because we are the same,
but because we are human—
and that's enough.
It always has been.

Hispanic America

You came before the borders, when the land stretched endlessly, a wild dance of sun and soil from the Rio Grande to the Atlantic shore.

Your hands pressed the earth, wrung life from desert stones, built the railroads that kissed the Pacific and pulled iron veins through mountain hearts.

You labored, nameless in the shadows, picking fruit under a sky too hot to care, stacking brick by brick the cities that rose against you. Your sweat stitched the flags of states that erased your name.

You crossed rivers and walls that called you stranger, sought refuge in a country that promised freedom with one hand and held a fist behind its back.

You brought music, words that sing, a legacy of languages twisted like vines, from the highlands of Peru to the streets of East LA, where you found the rhythm of your own pulse, created homes from thin air, family from the fragments.

You learned their laws, spoke their tongue, but kept your mother's voice in your heart, tucked the stories of ancestors beneath your children's pillows.

They called you illegal, as if you could be outlawed by lines on a map, as if your blood wasn't mixed into the clay that built their foundations.

They forgot that you were here first, conquistadors or not, your roots dug deep into this land before it had a name.

You earned your right to be here, in the fields of the Southwest, in the factories of the Midwest, in the classrooms and courtrooms, in the kitchen and the clinic, your legacy a thread woven into the very fabric of America.

You are the beat of the maracas, the hum of the mariachi's strings, the laughter shared in the language of two worlds.

You are the dream carried across deserts, the hope that refused to die when doors slammed in your face.

Hispanic America, you earned your place, not with papers or permission, but with the sweat of your brow, the breath of your ancestors, the strength of a spirit that bends, but never breaks.

You are America's heart, pumping life into its forgotten corners, a song that will not be silenced, a story that cannot be erased.

Latino America

You are the echo of ancient tongues, voices carried on the wind from the peaks of the Andes, the rain-soaked jungles of the Amazon, to the barrios where your children play in streets lined with the colors of home.

You are the map drawn without borders, a migration of hearts spanning oceans, deserts, streams—the Great Divide a line you crossed with dreams as wide as the sky, unwritten futures carried in your hands.

You are the rhythm of the conga, the sway of hips that remember the dances of ancestors, the pulse of salsa, bachata, cumbia, that shakes the silence of those who tried to erase you.

They call you foreign, yet you were here when the land was still raw, before cities rose like steel forests, before history was carved in English, you stood, nameless but not voiceless.

You picked the fruit from orchards that fed a nation, poured concrete in the midday sun, built homes where others found shelter, stood in kitchens behind the heat of the line, never seen, but felt in every bite.

You marched in the streets, banners held high, shouting in a language of resilience, fighting for a place at the table, a seat that you carved yourself from the wood of your own sweat and sacrifice.

Latino America, you are the strength of the mothers who braided stories into their children's hair, the fathers who bent but did not break, working hands raw, calloused by hope, cracked open by the weight of providing.

You are the bold laughter that fills the corners of rooms, the stories whispered late at night, passed down like heirlooms, each generation adding its own verse, its own beat.

They try to call you invisible, to mark you as an "other," but you are the sunrise over the fields, the sound of hammers at dawn, the prayers lifted on the smoke of backyard grills, the taste of tamales shared with neighbors who've become family.

You earned your right to be here, not with titles or decrees, but with the love you've rooted in this soil, the gardens you've planted in every heart that knows the warmth of your embrace.

Latino America, you are the voice that won't be silenced, the song that rises above the noise, the heartbeat of a land that beats to the rhythm of your resilience, that dances to the music of your legacy.

LGBTQ+ America

You are the rainbow before the storm clears,
a flash of color in a gray world,
standing in the truth after years of shadows.
You are the hidden hearts of history,
the quiet letters, the brave glances,
speaking when silence was easier.

You are Stonewall's bricks, the fists raised,
a riot that demanded to be seen, to be free,
in a world that tried to bury you in shame.
You are the kiss beneath moonlight,
the hand held openly, the march through prejudice,
turning streets into paths of pride.

You are the queens who wore courage with glitter,
the trans souls who faced their reflection
and found strength in their own truth.
You are the letters — L, G, B, T, Q —
a family bound by choice, a spectrum of light
in a world that sought to paint in black and white.

They tried to erase you,
but you rose from every slur, every law,
a voice that could not be silenced.

You cared for each other in times of crisis,
when the world looked away, you stood together,
finding strength in the hardest places.
You're changing minds, trying to change laws,
one conversation, one life at a time,
proving that you belong.

The America of the Native Americans

Before maps were drawn and flags unfurled,
this land already had a heartbeat,
a name whispered in winds that sang
through forests untouched by greed,
over plains where the buffalo roamed,
across waters that reflected the moon's quiet light.

You were the first to walk this earth,
to know the language of rivers,
to understand the song of the stars,
the cycle of seasons, the gift of rain,
the wisdom in a wolf's gaze,
the medicine in the roots that fed the soil.

You danced to the drum of the universe,
sang prayers to the sun's rise and fall,
your voices like the rustle of leaves,
a chorus with the breath of the land,
a harmony that knew no end.

You built no walls, but villages of stories,
where the firelight painted ancestors' faces
on the walls of memory.
Your history was carved in canyons,
etched in the bark of ancient trees,
woven into the fabric of the night sky.

Then came the strangers,
who called this wilderness,
who saw your way of life
and claimed it as their discovery,
who planted stakes in the ground
as if the earth could be owned
by anything but its own roots.

They broke treaties like the twigs of a fire,
pushed you from the land that held your ancestors' bones,
made you ghosts in your own homeland,
but you did not vanish.
Your spirit stayed, a river running deep,
hidden beneath the surface of their history books,
unwritten but not unremembered.

You are still here, in the beating wings of the eagle,
the smoke that rises from sacred fires,
the voices that speak your truth in council,
the songs sung by grandmothers
who have survived it all and still pass on
the stories of the old ways,
the tales of how the earth once was.

You fight to protect what is left,
to hold onto the land they called wild,
but you know it as mother,
know it as home,
know it as the first gift given to all.

The America of the Native Americans,
the America that breathes in tune with the trees,
the streams that know your ancestors' names,
the stones that hold your stories still,
the America that cannot be erased
by borders or battles,
for it lives in the spirit of the land,
in the heartbeat of the earth,
in the roots that grow deeper,
even when the surface is scorched.

Black America

You are the deep roots of a mighty oak,
buried in soil rich with the blood of ancestors,
tangled through time, pushing upward,
toward the light that once seemed
too far to reach.

You were brought here in chains,
shackled to the darkness of a ship's hold,
sold like the earth's own dust,
a life reduced to a number,
a name erased by the crack of a whip.
But they could not erase your spirit,
could not break what was already unbreakable,
the fire of your soul burning through the ash of despair.

You built America's fields,
your hands pulling cotton under a sun
that gave no mercy,
your sweat a silent rebellion
against the cries of "property" and "slave."
You sang hymns that flew above the plantations,
notes carried on the wind,
a chorus of freedom,
a coded message hidden in plain sight.

You walked through the fires of Jim Crow,
stood your ground on streets lined with hatred,
marched for the right to be seen,
to be heard, to be human,
to claim the birthright that was always yours
but written out of history's pages.
You gave voice to the voiceless,
from the pulpit, from the podium,
from the very back of the bus
to the steps of the Capitol.

Your music gave rhythm to this land,
from the gospel that lifted hearts to the heavens
to the blues that poured out of Mississippi's veins,
to jazz that broke free, improvising a new language,
to hip-hop that rose from the asphalt,
a declaration that you would not be silenced.

You are the poets who spoke truth to power,
the artists who painted freedom in every shade,
the dreamers who saw a world beyond the cage,
who refused to believe the lie
that you could be anything less than greatness.

Black America, you are the resilience
of the grandmother who rocked her child to sleep
with stories of kings and queens,
the strength of the father who took two jobs
to give his children a future,
the hope in the eyes of the boy on the corner
who imagines a world without fear,
the power in the voice of the girl who says,
"I am enough."

You are the civil rights that were fought for,
the progress that was hard-won,
the justice that is still demanded,
the promise of a dream not yet fulfilled.
You stand on the shoulders of giants,
your history carved in stone and sung in churches,
your struggle a bridge built over rivers of tears,
leading to a tomorrow you have not yet seen
but know is coming.

Black America, you earned your place,
with every step in the march,
with every note of the song,
with every drop of sweat and blood,
with every prayer whispered in the night.

You are America's heart and conscience,
the beat that moves us forward,
the voice that calls us to be better,
a light that refuses to dim.
You are the freedom yet to come,
the dream yet to rise,
the spirit that cannot be chained.

White America

You crossed oceans with dreams and holy texts,
landing on shores already known, already sung.
You came seeking freedom, a better life,
sowing both liberty and conquest in equal measure,
building towns from timber and grit,
forging paths through forests and rivers,
planting the seeds of a nation.

With hands hardened by work and hearts filled with hope,
you shaped cities from stone and steel,
clearing fields, building farms, raising homes on new ground.
You tilled the soil, nourished it with sweat,
and grew a vision of prosperity
where fields of corn and wheat met the endless sky.

You believed the land was yours to claim,
yet for all the wood and iron you hammered into place,
for every track carved across mountains,
and every town built by riversides,
there was an echo—
a reminder that this land held ancient stories,
woven long before your footprints marked the ground.

You carried ideals, spoke of freedom and law,
drafted constitutions, declarations, pledges,
crafted a framework that held a promise,
even when the lines were narrow,
marked by fear and pride,
even when you struggled to extend the rights
you believed so fiercely in.

Your statues rose high, symbols of vision and endeavor,
but the winds of change began to stir,
began to question, to erode those heights,
reminding you that even stone must bend to time.

White America, you are a mix, a confluence of color—
not a blank slate, but a layered tapestry,
each brushstroke a blend of light and shadow,
a canvas painted with hands from many lands.
You are inventors and dreamers, builders and teachers,
farmers and factory workers, soldiers and scholars,

mothers and fathers who labored
to make something lasting from the ground up.

You are part of the story, but not the whole of it,
a thread woven with others, each color a voice,
each voice a vital note in the song of this place.
Your cities hum with the work of your hands,
the bridges you built span rivers, connecting places,
the railroads you laid stretch across the nation,
binding distant states into a single heartbeat.

This land is shared, a history mirrored in light and shadow.
Your place here is earned by work and legacy,
by dreams stitched into the American fabric—
but the future will be defined by how you choose to see,
by the hands you join, by the voices you welcome,
by the willingness to listen and to learn.

For the true strength of America lies in unity,
in the richness of its diverse voices,
in the confluence of colors that together form its heart.
White America, remember the path you carved,
but look to the road ahead,
for there is still work to do,
a legacy to broaden, a promise to fulfill.

Asian America

You came from the East,
where the sun rises, to where it sets—
China, Japan, India, Korea, Vietnam, the Philippines,
a constellation of places,
cultures layered like rice paper, translucent and strong.
You sailed across the Pacific,
crossed deserts and mountains,
stood at Angel Island, a beacon
against the golden edge of America's dream.

In the railroads and gold mines, you built tracks
with the sweat of your ancestors,
laid the steel spine of this country
from coast to coast, from sea to shining sea.
The ground beneath your feet—
hard earth, harsh laws—
banned you, interned you, painted you as foreign.
But you stayed.
Your hands planted the seeds of vineyards,
your fingers sewed the silk of California's harvest.

Asian America, your voices blend—
Mandarin and Hindi, Tagalog and Tamil, Korean and Vietnamese—
a thousand dialects of resilience.
You carved a Chinatown in every city,
a Little Saigon, a Koreatown,
gathering stories of survival,
small businesses, quiet heroics,
family recipes passed like prayer.

You are doctors, scientists, poets, engineers,
dreamers and strivers, students burning
the midnight oil, coding the future.
You are the artists who write new lines
of what it means to be American,
the activists demanding a seat at the table,
telling the stories
of Vincent Chin and Maya Lin, of Yuri Kochiyama,
the nurse, the farmer, the undocumented,
who make America whole.

We owe you the flavors that spice our melting pot—

sesame oil and soy, the sharp tang of kimchi,
the sweet burn of Szechuan peppercorns.
Your music, a lute and a hip-hop beat,
bridges the Pacific, bridges our hearts.

You are more than a model, more than a myth—
you are woven into the fabric,
threads of silk and steel,
unbreakable in your quiet strength.

Asian America, I see you standing,
unbent, like bamboo in a storm,
rooted in ancestral soil
yet growing toward the light
of a country still learning
to see you,
to know you,
to embrace you
as its own.

Middle Eastern America

You arrived in waves,
with the sunbaked dust of deserts still clinging
to your shoes, the taste of pomegranate and olives
lingering on your lips.
You came from lands of ancient stories,
where the Nile, Tigris, and Euphrates
once cradled the first dreams of humanity.
You brought the call to prayer in your heart,
the chants of churches in your memories,
the dance of a thousand languages
spoken across the crossroads of the world.

Middle Eastern America,
you are the merchants and the poets,
the scientists and the storytellers.
You carved out a place in Dearborn and Paterson,
in the shadows of skyscrapers,
among the bright lights of new cities—
you built stores that smell of fresh bread and cardamom,
cafes where strong coffee burns like home in a cup.

You came seeking refuge,
fleeing the bombs that cracked open the earth,
the regimes that silenced voices.
You found new soil here,
planted your roots deep,
and grew gardens of jasmine and mint
in front yards overlooked by neighbors
who once called you stranger.

But they don't know you,
not really.
They see a face, a name they can't pronounce,
hear the echo of a language that sounds foreign—
but they don't know
the warmth of your table,
the sweetness of your dates and figs,
the songs you sing softly to your children at night,
the prayers you whisper under your breath
for a peace that feels like a distant memory.

You are doctors saving lives,

engineers sketching bridges,
teachers, taxi drivers, professors of ancient history,
telling stories of lands that once held the world's wisdom
in their hands.
You are Muslim, Christian, Jew—
faiths intertwined like vines,
the script of your holy books
written in the curves of Arabic calligraphy.

You have built your own mosques here,
churches with stained glass that tells new stories,
synagogues where the old songs rise again.
You dance at weddings,
the beat of the doumbek mixing with the heartbeat of America,
a rhythm that pulses through the streets
from Brooklyn to Los Angeles.

Middle Eastern America,
you know what it is to be both feared and unseen,
to be a symbol in someone else's story,
to be asked where you come from,
as if this place is not yours too.
You carry the weight of wars that are not your own,
the burden of headlines and sound bites,
the sideways glances in airports,
the suspicion that lingers like smoke.

But you are more than the sum of what they see—
you are the laughter that rises
from family dinners stretching long into the night,
the poetry that spills from your hands,
the resilience that grows in your bones.
You are the voice that joins the American chorus,
not always in harmony,
but always singing your own true song.

Middle Eastern America,
you are the bridge and the river,
the hands that hold both East and West.
You are the scent of cumin on a summer breeze,
the bright scarves that flash like sunlight,
the deep eyes that remember a thousand years of history.
You are here, now,

woven into the fabric of this land,
part of the patchwork,
adding your own rich thread to the story
of what it means to be American.

Female America

She rises early, before the sun,
long before the engines of industry hum,
before the news anchors speak,
she is already working—
in the fields, the offices, the classrooms,
at the kitchen table with a pencil and a prayer,
the small, fierce light of morning
held in her hands like a promise.

She came here in petticoats and chains,
with a bonnet or a shaved head,
a slave ship's dark belly or a boat from across the sea,
she was an immigrant, a mother,
a suffragette marching down the avenue,
a flapper shedding the corset,
a factory girl building the bones of a new world.
She worked the soil, tilled it with her bare hands,
picked cotton and coffee beans,
nursed the sick, taught the young,
stood at the front lines with her heart on her sleeve.

Female America, you are the story
that wasn't written in history books,
the footnote that carried the weight of the main text.
You fought for the right to vote,
broke the chains of tradition,
tore down walls brick by brick—
sometimes in silence,
sometimes with a roar
that echoed through the chambers of power.

You are the voices—
Sojourner, Susan, Ida, Eleanor—
those who could not speak
but still made their voices heard,
those who held placards, raised fists,
sang lullabies and anthems,
knitted socks for soldiers, signed petitions,
and walked out of kitchens
into boardrooms and battlefields.

You are the heartbeat of movements,

from Seneca Falls to Selma,
from the streets of Tehran to the halls of Congress.
You've bled for this land,
carried its children,
cried out in the pain of labor and loss,
wept into the soil when your sons did not return.

Female America, I see you in the hard gaze of a woman
who will not look away,
in the hand that rocks the cradle and the hand
that passes laws, heals wounds,
writes novels, codes software, and paints dreams.
You are the scientist who mapped the stars,
the poet who redefined freedom,
the girl who stood up in a classroom
and said "No more."

You are more than a mother, a daughter, a sister—
you are the breath between words,
the echo of the past and the pulse of the future,
a river that runs deep, carving the canyon,
turning the wheel of history.
You are the laugh that holds sorrow,
the tear that cleanses,
the fierce embrace of one who loves
and refuses to let go.

Female America, you wear a thousand faces,
call a thousand names your own,
carry the scars and the joys
of a million stories untold.
You are the strength beneath the skyline,
the roots of the tallest trees,
the ground that holds us steady.

I see you standing there,
unshaken, with the weight of the world
in your hands,
lifting it like it's nothing,
like it's everything.

Male America

He stands tall at the edge of the wilderness,
an axe in his hand, the bark biting back.
He is the farmer turning earth,
the builder of barns and bridges,
squinting into the sun
as he lays the first brick,
hoisting steel beams skyward—
a skyline born from his roughened palms.

He came on ships that barely survived the sea,
from Europe, Africa, Asia, the islands—
penniless, shackled, seeking, escaping.
He was a boy soldier in blue and gray,
fighting brother against brother,
the dust of Gettysburg and Antietam
still clinging to his boots,
dreaming of a land not yet whole.

Male America, you are the cowboy on horseback,
the factory worker's calloused knuckles,
the miner's lantern, dim but determined
in the belly of the earth.
You drove the spikes into the transcontinental,
held the wheel of a Model T,
stood in breadlines,
filled the foxholes in Normandy,
a cigarette dangling from your lips,
the taste of fear and courage mingled.

You are fathers and sons,
grandfathers with stories spun into the night—
some true, some embellished—
but all told with the weight of a legacy
that can't be ignored.
You are the sweat on a laborer's brow,
the ink on a CEO's contract,
the protester's shout and the preacher's prayer,
the jazzman's fingers dancing across ivory keys
in a Harlem club at midnight.

Male America, I see you in the hero's journey,
from the plains of the Midwest to the streets of Detroit,

in the Silicon Valley coder's glare,
the poet's quiet words
etched into the margin of a notebook.
You are the maker of rules
and the breaker of them,
the architect of dreams
and sometimes the destroyer of them.

You fought for freedom,
but sometimes for power,
for glory, or for nothing at all
except the feel of your fist landing
and the hollow cheer of the crowd.
You've led armies and nations,
but stumbled, lost in your own shadow,
caught between what you were taught
and what you must learn.

Male America, you are more than Marlboro men
and Wall Street wolves,
more than quarterbacks and cowboys,
more than power suits and pocket knives.
You are the father at the breakfast table,
eyes lined with fatigue,
reading the paper,
worrying about what the world will hand his children.
You are the boy who wanted to be a hero,
the man who realized the price of it.

You carry the weight of generations,
the promise of what you could be,
the fear of failing it all.
You are the laughter echoing in the backyard,
the steady hand on a shoulder,
the rough voice that says, "It's going to be okay,"
even when you aren't sure.

Male America, I see you standing,
not as the rock but as the river—
carving your path through time,
sometimes raging, sometimes gentle,
shaping the land,
reflecting the sky.

You are the strength and the silence,
the storm and the stillness.
You are the question without an answer,
the bridge we walk on,
the road we follow,
the shadow and the light
of this ever-unfolding story.

Intergenerational America

From the first breath of a newborn's cry
to the last sigh of a life well-lived,
we are woven into the tapestry
of this land, each thread a story,
each life a moment stitched
into the fabric of the possible.

The young bring light to the morning,
their laughter ringing like church bells,
ideas as wild as the prairie sky,
beliefs like stones skipped across rivers,
disrupting the water but leaving ripples
that reach the farthest shore.

They run forward, impatient for change,
burning with a fire that could light the world,
or scorch it if we aren't careful
to guide them, hold them close
without holding them back.

The middle years, standing like strong oaks,
weathering storms of work and worry,
carrying the weight of dreams still building,
the steady hum of hands that create,
plan, nurture, and teach the young
to stand on shoulders of giants
they have yet to recognize.

We are the bridge between hope and history,
the engine of today's world,
our backs bent like the rivers
that carved out this country's bones,
our hearts the pulse of its beating chest.

And the elders, the roots sunk deep,
holding memories like sacred texts,
whispering the lessons of yesterday
in voices softened by time.

They have seen the rise and fall,
heard the echoes of wars and dances,
lived the decades that twist and turn

like mountain roads in morning fog.

They carry the wisdom of the earth itself,
remind us that progress is a slow waltz,
not a sprint, that the seeds we plant today
are sown in the fields they once plowed.

From young to old, from breath to dust,
we are linked in a chain unseen,
passed from hand to hand,
a great inheritance of love and loss,
of stories half-remembered,
of dreams that didn't end
but transformed into something new.

We are the children of the past,
the parents of the future,
and this moment is ours to tend,
to strengthen the links with kindness,
to mend what is frayed with understanding,
to honor those who came before
and make way for those yet to come.

This is our America—
not just the land beneath our feet,
but the space between each generation,
the bridge we must keep strong,
so the light of our shared journey
never fades, and the great chain
of being remains unbroken.

Today's Ghettoes

The concrete still crumbles,
but the people endure,
confined by invisible chains
that murmur, "This is your place—
beyond this line, you don't belong."

Poverty and prejudice, like rats immune to every cure,
scurry through each alleyway,
gnawing on the edges of progress,
surviving every gallant effort
to stamp them out for good.

Generations are born,
grow old, and die,
but the ghettos persist—
unbroken promises etched
into every brick and boarded window.

The rhetoric of justice fills the air,
but still, it doesn't penetrate these walls,
where dreams are stunted,
and futures are as fractured as the streets.

Hope slips like dust
through fingers grasping for better,
as the horizon remains ever distant,
like a mirage that disappears
the closer you come.

In the outskirts, trailer parks cling to dirt roads,
small-town homes sag, their paint peeled by time.
Urban blocks bleed the same aching poverty—
dilapidated houses on the edge of town,
staring into a future they know won't change.

Still, they wait and wonder,
if change will one day arrive,
or if this place—
this ghetto of the 21st century—
will forever stand, untouched by time,
a monument to a battle yet to be won.

Charleston's Dark Hour, June 17, 2015

The old church stood, white walls gleaming in the Southern sun,
Emanuel AME, a house of prayer, a sanctuary of hope.
Its doors were open wide, as they always had been—
welcoming hearts seeking solace, seeking God.
But one June night, the walls bled red,
stained by an unimaginable evil that stalked inside.

He sat with them, a wolf among the lambs,
listening to their prayers, their voices rising up,
unaware of the hatred seething just a few feet away.
He was Dylann Roof—unremarkable and young,
with pale skin, hollow eyes, a mind poisoned by lies,
believing in the twisted gospel of supremacy.

He came to silence their hymns,
to prove his worth to the ghosts of a confederacy long dead.
And when he rose, it was not to offer peace
but to unleash bullets that tore through flesh and bone,
ripped open dreams, splattered prayers on the walls—
turning a place of light into a tomb of darkness.

Nine lives extinguished in a hail of gunfire,
their blood soaking the sanctuary floor—
the Reverend Clementa Pinckney fell, his voice
forever stilled, while others, mothers and fathers,
brothers and sisters, felt the cold hand of death
wrap around them in what should have been a holy hour.

The aftermath was an open wound—
white walls marred by bullet holes and bloodstains,
the wooden pews silent witnesses to unfathomable grief.
Outside, the flowers piled up like fragile shields
against a history that kept repeating itself,
a history of burning crosses and shattered dreams.

A country watched in horror, but the horror was old,
a haunting that never seemed to leave,
like a shadow cast by a tree that once bore
strange fruit along its limbs.
The community wept, their cries echoing
through the cracked hearts of a nation that still bleeds.

Racism's ugly specter emerged from its pit,
howling in the face of progress, baring its teeth,
feeding on the embers of fear and ignorance.
And the shooter—born to the same land that birthed hope,
raised by a country that failed to kill the lie
that some lives are worth less than others—
took his belief in hate and turned it into a weapon.

Even now, years later, the wound is still raw.
The church stands—restored, but never the same,
for the spirits of the fallen linger in every shadow,
their names whispered in the sigh of every breeze.
The nation looks on, still grappling with the truth—
that in the land of the free, hatred festers like a wound,
and justice remains an unfinished hymn.

How many more times will we gather the shattered pieces,
speak the names of the dead like a prayer
that falls on deaf ears, while hatred slips
through the cracks of our fractured union?
When will we confront the ugliness in our own reflection,
and tear down the lies we tell ourselves,
that we are a land of liberty and justice for all?

No, not while the stain of Charleston remains,
not while hatred wears the face of the familiar,
and bullets find homes in holy places.
For as long as we allow the seeds of bigotry to grow,
we will be forced to reap what has been sown,
and the bells of Emanuel will toll—
not just for the nine who died,
but for a nation still clinging to its ghosts.

Harris's American Crossroads

A woman stood steady, poised,
eyes lifted, voice calm as water
over smooth stones, an even hand
against the tide's push. She spoke
with resolve shaped by struggle,
words polished in law's tempered light.

She called for unity, for the patching
of America's open seams, the stitching
of values many hold dear. Yet,
in her vision, a storm brewed, quiet
beneath the promise of calm.
In her crowd, they gathered,
hopeful, mistrustful,
some drawn to her strength,
others wary of the past she wore—
law and order's weight, progress
measured in cautious steps.

America, she had said,
let us rise together,
and yet the crowd's hopeful voices split,
like a road parting in two directions,
the center line fraying underfoot.
For some, she was justice renewed,
the promise of light and balance.
For others, she embodied
an order they did not trust,
her voice too soft, her promise too still
to quiet their restless fear.

And in the end, she did not win.
The path she carved, a hopeful plea,
left untraveled, as voices rose
for another way, her vision passed by,
her promise yet unfulfilled.
She stood as paradox,
strength veiled in calm,
determination housed in quiet resolve.

Her campaign faded, her words linger,
as the country pondered what shape
it might yet take—
and what it may never be again.

Trump's American Blaze

In the heart of a divided nation, a man rose, familiar yet renewed, his voice a clarion call to those who felt unseen, unheard, forgotten.

He spoke of strength, of reclaiming a past painted in hues of greatness, igniting flames in the hearts of those yearning for simpler times.

The ballots cast, the verdict clear, a victory forged in the crucible of discontent and desire, ushering in an era of singular power.

With the executive, legislative, and judicial branches aligned, the delicate dance of checks and balances now a memory, a cautionary tale.

In this blaze of unity, the risk of overreach looms large, as the flames of ambition threaten to consume the very fabric of democracy.

Yet within this conflagration, a call emerges, clear and resolute: to temper courage with wisdom, might with compassion, to navigate the path ahead with ethics and honor as our guides.

For in the ashes of division, the seeds of healing lie dormant, waiting for the gentle rain of understanding and unity.

Let us remember the beauty of democracy, a tapestry woven from diverse threads, and strive to mend the fractures, to rebuild with care and intention.

As the embers of this American blaze glow in the twilight, may we find the strength to heal, to unite, to forge a future worthy of the ideals we hold dear.

George Floyd

His breath was taken,
but his name lives on,
murmured in the streets,
painted on walls,
a reminder of how fragile life can be
when skin is seen as a threat.

Eight minutes,
forty-six seconds,
and the world shook,
because in that time,
we all saw
what has been happening
for far too long.

The ground trembles
with the weight of his absence,
but his name has become
a rallying cry for justice.

Proud Boys on January 6, 2021

They stormed the steps,
clad in the colors of a nation,
but carrying hate in their hearts.

Flags waved,
but they weren't for unity—
they were for power,
for a version of America
built on exclusion,
built on fear.

And as they broke the walls,
they broke something deeper—
the fragile thread
that holds democracy together,
now frayed,
now torn.

The Plight of Native Americans

The land beneath their feet,
once theirs,
now taken,
now scarred.

Promises broken,
treaties ignored—
the story of America
written in the tears of those
whose ancestors roamed free.

Today, the fight continues,
for recognition,
for dignity,
for land,
for the right to be
on soil that remembers
their songs.

Fault Lines

In the land of bright stars and fading dreams,
two voices rise, split at the core,
each singing a tune of freedom
but marching to a different beat.

One hand clutches the past,
a proud tradition, rooted and firm,
where country means heritage, faith, a name,
an inheritance held close, blood-red, deep as veins.
They speak of order, strength, a nation secure,
of borders that hold, values that stay—
conserving what's built, wary of change,
believing, perhaps, that what was
is what should be.

Across the divide, others gather,
unfurled banners of progress,
seeking a future that feels
just out of reach,
a vision of hands open, voices raised
for justice, equality, a redefined land
that bends, sways, and stretches to fit
the many who make it whole.
They speak of freedom anew,
a nation that shifts, roots unbound,
believing in change like a river
carving its way.

But both fear the other's world:
one side sees chaos, walls crumbling,
a loss of place,
where identity blurs,
and dreams once steady falter.
The other sees cages, doors locked tight,
a nation hardened, closed to the breath
of new life, turned inward
as the world spins on.

They stand in the same soil,
each rooted deep,
yet neither can see beyond the horizon
of their own beliefs,

and the earth beneath them trembles,
cracks spreading wide,
a chasm fed by fear and the weight of wounds
long buried.

An election looms,
and with it, a reckoning—
not just of ballots and votes,
but of what it means to be free
in a land that's bound
by more than blood and borders.

Will the voices find a bridge,
or will they shatter the ground they share,
as neighbors turn from one another,
forgetting, maybe,
that fault lines only deepen
when the earth stands still.

Today's Immigration Politics

In the mosaic of our nation, each tile tells a story— some of hope, others of fear, many still unwritten.

Voices rise, calling for walls to mark the boundaries of belonging, seeking to define who may enter and who must remain outside.

Others advocate for open doors, embracing the weary travelers who arrive with dreams and burdens unseen.

Between these poles lies a spectrum, where debates over deportation and sanctuary intertwine, each argument a thread in the complex fabric of policy.

We grapple with the shadows of those who bring harm, acknowledging that safety demands vigilance, that those who flee justice find no haven here.

Yet, we must also see the faces of the persecuted, the hands that reach out from across borders, seeking refuge from storms we cannot fathom.

In this discourse, let us balance the scales of compassion and caution, weighing human dignity against the imperatives of security.

May we recognize the humanity in each soul that seeks our shores, while safeguarding the principles that define our collective home.

For in the end, the question remains: how do we honor the legacy of a nation built by many hands, while protecting the sanctuary we've come to cherish?

Let us tread this path with care, acknowledging the trade-offs, embracing the unknown, and striving for a future where justice and mercy walk hand in hand.

The War Between Extremes

The middle ground,
once firm,
has disappeared.
Now, it's a battlefield,
where the right and the left
shout from their trenches,
but no one hears.
The space between
has grown so wide,
it feels like no one
wants to cross it.
And as the war rages on,
we forget
that there's a country
caught in the middle,
a people waiting for peace,
waiting for reason.

Have You Been to Pine Ridge? I Have.

Have you been to Pine Ridge? I have.
Do you know the dust that clings to the soles of your shoes,
the hollow eyes of children,
the lines etched in the faces of the old ones—
each groove a story of promises broken,
of land stripped bare,
of a people left with nothing but memory?

They say Wounded Knee still weeps.
A quiet place, but not silent.
The earth remembers,
even when the world forgets.
And the wind—oh, the wind—
it carries whispers of ghosts,
of ancestors who danced with the buffalo,
who lived in rhythm with the land
before the treaties,
before the rifles,
before everything was taken.

Have you seen the children?
Their laughter—rare, brittle—
bouncing off broken trailers and cracked roads,
where hope gets swallowed by hunger
and dreams die in the shadow of liquor stores.
What future is there in a place where poverty
wraps itself around you like a second skin?
The schools teach them words that don't belong,
teach them to forget who they are,
teach them to survive in a world
that doesn't see them, doesn't care.

And the elders…
The elders sit in silence,
watching the slow decay of all they fought to preserve.
The sacred ways, the stories, the songs—
slipping through their fingers
like sand in a river.
They've seen too much, these old ones.
They remember when the land was still theirs,
when the rivers ran clean,
when they could look at the sky

and see freedom.
Now they look at their grandchildren
and see a different kind of captivity.

What have we done?
We build casinos and call it progress,
build pipelines and call it necessity.
We carve up their land,
again and again,
intruding upon the sacred,
telling them it's for the greater good,
as if our good was ever theirs.

Have you walked the dirt roads of Pine Ridge?
Have you seen the desperation in the eyes of a mother
whose children go to bed hungry?
The addiction that gnaws at the edges of a father's soul,
trying to drown out the pain,
the rage,
the sorrow.

Wounded Knee was not the end—
it was only the beginning.
The blood of their ancestors still stains this earth,
still cries out for justice,
but we've turned a deaf ear,
shut our eyes to the truth of their suffering.

They took the land,
they took the buffalo,
they took the language,
the spirit,
the fire.
But the people, they remain.
They endure,
though the world pretends not to see them.

We drive past,
forgetting they are still here—
struggling, surviving,
on land that no longer nourishes,
on dreams that have been burned.

Have you been to Pine Ridge? I have.
Have you seen the beauty still living there?
In the children's eyes, despite the hunger,
in the elders' stories, despite the sorrow.

Have you felt the spirit of a people
who refuse to die,
who hold on,
generation after generation,
who, against all odds,
are still here,
still fighting,
still dreaming of a day when their land is theirs again,
when their voices are heard,
when the earth remembers its original songs?

Yes, Pine Ridge is broken,
but it is not lost.
There is strength in the roots,
though the tree has been scarred.
There is power in remembering,
in keeping alive what was almost taken away.

Have you been to Pine Ridge?
If you go,
listen closely.
The land has stories to tell.
The people have a history that breathes,
and it is not finished yet.

Book Banning

In the quiet of classrooms,
stories are being silenced.
Books that once opened worlds
are now being closed,
shelved,
banned.
Knowledge, too,
is under attack,
because truth is a threat
to those who fear it.
But the stories remain,
whispered in the corners,
passed hand to hand,
because the power of words
cannot be caged.

Systemic Racism

It's not always loud,
not always obvious.
It's in the cracks of the system,
in the spaces where decisions are made
but not everyone is at the table.
It's in the policies,
in the laws,
in the unspoken rules
that keep the doors closed
to some,
while others walk freely through.
It's the weight you feel
without seeing it,
the invisible hand
that holds you down.

The Failure of Faith

Faith was supposed to heal,
to build bridges,
to unite.
But too often,
it builds walls—
walls made of steel,
of doctrine,
of belief so rigid
it cannot bend.
Instead of welcoming,
it excludes,
and those seeking justice,
seeking fairness,
find only a closed door
with a lock of judgment.

What Elections Have Become in America

In the heart of democracy, elections pulse, the lifeblood of a nation's voice, each vote a heartbeat, each ballot a testament to freedom's call.

Yet shadows creep upon this sacred rite, threats to its integrity loom large: disinformation's web entangles truth, casting doubt where certainty should reside, while foreign hands, unseen, reach in, seeking to sway the course of destiny.

Civility, once the cornerstone of discourse, now crumbles under the weight of division, as voices rise not in debate, but in derision, and the common ground erodes beneath our feet.

Complex issues, reduced to soundbites, nuance lost in the clamor for attention, candidates molded to fit the mold, their depths obscured by the glare of the spotlight.

Elections, doors to possibility, swing open to progress, or close upon regression, each outcome a step toward unity or fracture, the path ahead uncertain, yet ours to choose.

Let us reclaim the sanctity of this process, restore the grace of respectful exchange, embrace the complexity of our shared challenges, and honor the power vested in our collective will.

For in the act of choosing, we define ourselves, and the future we bequeath to those who follow, a legacy written in the ink of our intentions, etched upon the canvas of a nation's soul.

The Issues That Unite and Divide Us

We gather around the dinner table of this nation,
with plates full of opinions,
forks sharp with certainty—
immigration, the economy, social justice, education—
we argue and dream with our mouths full,
hard to listen when the noise of our own voices
drowns out the echo of others.

You speak of immigration as a border to guard,
a wall to build, a line drawn in the sand—
I see it as a river,
carrying those who long for a chance
to drink from the same well of hope.
We build our visions of America
on different blueprints,
the pencil marks of fear and freedom
smudged together.

The economy rises and falls like a breath,
and we argue over who deserves
the deepest gulp of air—
the rich and the poor,
the makers and takers,
the bootstrap believers and those drowning
in debt's relentless tide.
We measure success in skyscrapers or soup kitchens,
count our worth in stock tickers or sleepless nights.
But the American Dream was written in cursive,
a promise we struggle to read
with calloused fingers.

Social justice hangs in the air like smoke—
some choke on it, others breathe it in deep,
saying it smells like revolution,
like change, like the first rain after a drought.
But we wear our politics like blindfolds,
see what we choose to see:
the handcuffs, the protests, the courtrooms,
the unspoken biases, the tears we ignore
because they aren't falling from our own eyes.

On education, we debate what to teach our children,
whose history gets written into the textbooks,
whose voices echo in their classrooms.
The government we built to run this house—
some say it's too big,
some say it's too small,
but few of us are willing
to roll up our sleeves and fix the leaking pipes,
patch the roof, sweep the floors.

We hold abortion in our hands like a live wire,
an issue that shocks us into silence or shouts,
a question of life, a question of choice,
a battle fought in courts and clinics,
with signs held high,
but who holds the hand of the woman
caught between belief and body?

Climate change and the environment
are the clouds gathering overhead—
some of us see a storm coming,
others look away, blinded by the bright sun
of fossil fuels, the promise of profit.
We drill and burn,
watching the smoke rise like prayers,
while the ice melts, the seas rise,
and our children wonder
if we saw it coming at all.

Energy choices divide us,
split us like an atom—
solar, wind, coal, oil—
we fight over the veins of the earth,
forgetting that the blood we spill
belongs to us all.

What does it mean to be rich?
Is it the mansion, the yacht,
the bank account with too many zeros to count?
Or is it the dinner table crowded with family,
the laugh lines on your face,
the peace of a good night's sleep?

We define poverty by the number of dollars,
but the soul can be bankrupt too,
stripped of dignity, starved of dreams.

Economic and social mobility,
the ladder we're told to climb,
each rung a promise that if you work hard enough,
you can reach the stars.
But we look up and see rungs missing,
the wood cracked and splintered,
while some stand at the top,
never knowing the weight of the climb.

Healthcare, foreign relations,
the balance of power—
we tug at the rope in this endless tug-of-war,
men and women pulling from different ends,
arguing about gender roles,
who belongs in what box,
while life continues outside the lines
we've drawn so carefully.

We get caught up in stereotypes,
swallowed by sound bites,
pinned down by headlines that flatten us
into caricatures—
liberal, conservative, right, left,
patriot, protester, believer, heretic—
we wear our labels like armor,
shielding ourselves from the truth
of our own complexities.

We see each other as threats,
not as fellow travelers on this road,
our inability to listen the greatest wall of all.
We don't understand that belief can bend,
that authority can be questioned,
that truth can be held in two hands,
not clenched in a single fist.

If we don't find a way
to meet in the space between our words,

if we can't learn to share this table,
taste each other's tears,
swallow each other's hopes,
then we are doomed—
a family divided,
a country on the brink,
the foundation cracking beneath us
as we argue about who gets the biggest slice
of a pie that's already crumbling.

Rise of the Klan and White Supremacy in the 21st Century

They wear no hoods now,
no burning crosses to light the night—
their faces are bare,
smiling in suits,
in the glare of cameras,
on the steps of courthouses,
in the chambers of power.

But still, the shadow lingers,
deep and wide,
the Klan is not gone—
it has only changed its clothes.

In whispers and slogans,
they declare themselves "patriots,"
their flags waving,
not the stars and bars,
but symbols of a different fight,
codes etched in pixels,
in online threads that twist the truth
into something monstrous,
something hidden.

It's in the rallies
where torches rise once more,
not in backwoods but in cities,
marching in the open,
chanting ancient hatreds
as if time has stood still.
"Unite the Right," they call it—
but what they seek
is to divide,
to fracture,
to keep the lines drawn
between us.

It's in the school boards,
where history is rewritten,
scrubbed clean of the blood
that built this nation.
They call it pride,
but it's erasure—

a refusal to see
what lies beneath the surface.

It's in the quiet corners,
where hands shake behind closed doors,
laws passed with smiles
that hold the weight of something darker.
Voter suppression,
gerrymandering,
they carve out the future,
making sure the game
is always rigged in their favor.

And in the streets,
it shows its teeth—
Charlottesville,
Kenosha,
a church in Charleston,
in Ohio, downtown Springfield,
a grocery store in Buffalo.
The bullets still fly,
the hatred still burns,
and though they claim innocence,
their fingers are never far
from the trigger.

But it's not just the blatant,
not just the swastikas
spray-painted on synagogue doors.
It's in the casual conversations,
the jokes shared in whispers,
the way people turn their heads
when a white man says,
"We need to take our country back."

It's in the silence
that follows these words,
the quiet acceptance
that lets the darkness
grow.

They're not wearing hoods now,
but their message is the same—

to build a world
where only some belong,
where the color of skin
is a barrier,
a dividing line.
They've learned how to hide it
in plain sight,
but it's there,
growing.

White supremacy hasn't faded,
it's adapted,
slipped into the cracks
of our institutions,
our systems,
our streets.
And if we don't see it,
if we don't name it,
it will rise,
higher than ever,
until the flames
once hidden,
once denied,
burn through us all.

Defenders and Disruptors: A Presidential Chronicle

Kennedy, with his young face and old vision,
stood at the brink of nuclear fire,
and faced the Cuban missiles down—
his steady hand a shield
against the chaos of a world in fear.

Johnson, weathered by the struggles of the South,
signed the Civil Rights Act,
broke the chains of segregation,
and though the war tore him apart,
he raised the hope of a Great Society
in the cracks of division.

Nixon, flawed and secretive,
still went to China,
opened the gates of diplomacy,
bridging the chasm of Cold War fear—
a gesture of peace in a divided globe.

Ford, who pardoned a scandal's ghost,
knew the nation needed healing more than vengeance,
and with a simple act of mercy,
he tried to bind the wounds
of a fractured American soul.

Carter, soft-spoken yet firm in faith,
brokered peace at Camp David,
sat with enemies and made them shake hands,
believing in the power of dialogue
over the sharp edge of the sword.

Reagan, with his actor's voice,
stood at Berlin's wall and called it down—
"Mr. Gorbachev, tear down this wall!"
He rekindled a belief in American power,
a voice that pierced the iron curtain.

Bush, the elder statesman,
crafted a coalition in the Gulf,
stood against a tyrant's invasion,
and in quiet diplomacy,
navigated the end of the Cold War

with a careful hand.

Clinton, saxophone and all,
built bridges across party lines,
expanded the economy's reach,
and fought for a peace
in the rocky hills of the Balkans,
defending democracy in foreign lands.

Bush, the son, marked by 9/11's scar,
stood on rubble with a bullhorn,
and though the wars would shadow his legacy,
in those moments of dust and grief,
he became the voice of a wounded nation,
vowing freedom's fight.

Obama, with his voice of hope,
led us through a crisis of our making,
stabilized a crumbling economy,
and with steady steps,
took out a terror's face—
Bin Laden, a strike for justice and memory.

Trump, brash and brazen,
tore at the seams of tradition,
yet in his storm,
awoke a new wave of civic engagement—
for or against,
he brought democracy's debates
into every kitchen table conversation.

Biden, with a father's heart and steady hands,
entered in a storm, the nation divided, aching.
He brought vaccines, a chance for healing,
spoke of unity as fires of discord burned.
He stood with allies against autocrats' threats,
pulled us back from the edge of chaos,
a calm voice in the noise of a fractured era.

America called for change in 2024, a return to the familiar,
bringing Trump back to the White House once more.
He swept in with promises to undo and rebuild,
tearing down the past, reshaping the present.

Policies overturned, a new vision imposed,
as the country followed, divided yet yearning—
carried forward to a new, uncertain chapter.

Each man, imperfect,
a chapter in the story of a nation,
defenders in their own way,
struggling with the weight of the office,
holding the fragile line
of freedom and democracy
with human hands.

America's Second Civil War

It simmers beneath the surface,
a war without battlegrounds,
but with casualties just the same.
A war of ideology,
of hate and wealth,
of who deserves a place
in this fractured land.
The lines are drawn,
not by geography,
but by belief—
a refusal to see the other side,
a desire for power
that drowns out the call
for humanity.

The signs are there,
etched in steel and stone,
in armored thoughts and whispered lies.
Misinformation spreads like wildfire,
intentional, sharp,
designed to divide,
to twist the truth until it no longer shines.
Disinformation follows,
an echo in the chambers of power,
where truth is drowned
by the clamor of those
who want to own it.

We've seen the guns,
the unfettered access,
in the hands of men and women,
in the church pews,
in the classroom aisles.
We've seen them in the White House,
on the steps of Congress,
where decisions are no longer made
with words alone.
Authoritarianism creeps in
like a shadow,
masked as order,
masked as safety,
but it's fear that drives it forward,

and the people nod,
believing the lie.

There is meanness here,
not just in the streets,
but in the voices of those
who preach from the pulpit,
who teach in the classroom,
who sit on the boards of education
and decide which books we're allowed to read.
There is hatred here,
not just on the fringes,
but in the workplace,
in the dinner conversations,
passed from one generation to the next
as though it were inheritance,
as though it were truth.

The guns—
they are everywhere.
Loaded and waiting,
for someone to pull the trigger,
for someone to take the first step
over the line we've drawn.
And all the while,
the war simmers beneath,
growing hotter,
waiting for a spark.

Unless we let go
of these armored beliefs,
this grip on tyrannical thoughts,
the lies we've been fed,
the war will rise.
Unless we suppress the voices
of authoritarianism,
of cultural meanness,
of hatred that digs into the soil
like roots refusing to be pulled,
the war will come.

It won't be fought
in fields or trenches—

it will be fought in our homes,
in the streets,
in the places we thought were safe.
It will tear through the halls of Congress,
the White House,
the places where democracy
once had a chance to breathe.

We are teetering on the edge,
one step away from the point
where there is no turning back.
Unless we loosen our hold
on the need to control,
to dominate,
to be right,
the war will not stay simmering—
it will boil over,
and when it does,
there will be no winners,
only the ashes
of what could have been.

The Silent March of Time

We never see it coming,
the slow drift,
the way days fold into years
until everything we thought was firm
begins to slip.

History isn't just in books;
it's in the cracks of the pavement,
the wrinkles of our elders' hands,
the words we whisper
when the room goes quiet.

There are wars no one remembers,
laws no one recalls were passed,
faces that once led the charge
now blurred at the edges,
but time keeps moving.
It doesn't wait for us to catch up.

We spend our days
building monuments
to things that might not last,
writing speeches that fade with the wind,
thinking we know
how this story will end.

But sometimes,
just sometimes,
we forget—
time isn't a straight line.
It curves,
it doubles back,
it surprises us
with memories we thought we'd buried.

And maybe, just maybe,
one day we'll look up,
and see
that the future we've been marching toward
was right here
in the footsteps
we've already left behind.

The Things We Refuse to See

Nobody wants to lose what they have,
so we cling tightly to the edges of comfort,
wrap ourselves in the worn blanket of habit.
We tolerate injustice like a dull ache—
nagging, persistent, but not unbearable enough
to disturb the quiet of our own small lives.

Unfairness slips into the cracks
of our everyday, lives lived by rote,
and we turn our heads away from the ugliness
that blooms like weeds at the edges of our vision.
Hatred, that ancient sickness, festers beneath the surface,
masked by polite words and silent indifference.

For most of us, the truth is buried so deep
we've forgotten how to dig it out,
forgotten how to turn our eyes inward,
to see the shadows that move within us.
Prejudice is built into the bones—
inherited, ingrained, fed to us in fragments
until it hardens into stone.

And when it rears its ugly head,
when it shows itself plainly, naked, grotesque,
we avert our gaze, refuse to name it.
It is easier to pretend it belongs to someone else,
to other places, other people, other times.
But no, we are all possessed—
demon-haunted in our indifference,
choosing to guard our tiny piece of the universe
as if nothing else matters.

The human race has waged war
on itself for centuries, on every continent,
in every age—hatred, injustice,
that self-righteous certainty that we are right,
that we are better, that others must be less.
We make ourselves bigger by making others smaller,
forgetting that to diminish one is to diminish all.

And here we are, even now,
allowing the extremes to dictate our lives—

in politics, in economics, in every breath we take.
We've given power to the loudest voices,
to the ones who say it's okay to hate,
that violence is a right, that freedom means
we can crush what we don't understand.

But there are some things we must not protect,
must not cloak in the guise of liberty—
prejudice is not a freedom to cherish,
hatred should not find shelter in any constitution,
nor any holy book, nor any scientific claim
that says it's fine to be the way we are.

We are not bound to this fate,
not condemned to repeat history's mistakes,
to let the next war—civil or otherwise—
consume us all, our bodies piled like ash
on the pyre of our own making.
We can do better; we must.

It is time to look inward, to unearth the shadows
that dwell within us, to confront the demons
we've so long refused to name.
For there is work to be done,
and it begins in the heart—each heart—
where the hardest battles are fought,
and where change is born, not in a roar,
but in the quiet realization that we don't
have to be the way we are.

The things we refuse to see,
we must see.
The things we protect that should not be protected,
we must let go.
For the cost of our blindness is too great,
and the next war will not spare us,
no matter which side we think we stand on.

We Can No Longer Pretend Everything Will Be All Right

We can no longer pretend,
not if we keep turning away,
eyes downcast,
hoping the storm will pass
without a single move toward shelter.
We can no longer pretend everything will be all right
if we are unwilling to change,
unwilling to bend where the broken pieces lie.

The time for silence has passed—
now, the time is for collaboration,
for hands outstretched across the divide,
for compromises forged in the fires
of a better tomorrow,
for a government rebuilt
on the ashes of what we once believed
was unshakable.
The pillars of democracy,
of justice and freedom,
are cracked and crumbling.
We must rise,
rebuild with every piece of truth we can find,
before they fall into dust.

We can no longer pretend it will all be fine
while the rich carve out their empires,
dictating how we live,
how our children learn,
how the future is molded by those
whose pockets are too deep to feel the weight
of the decisions they make.
We cannot let religious fervor replace reason,
cannot allow dogma to silence science.
The truth is burning beneath our feet,
and we must act
before it consumes us whole.

We can no longer pretend that leaders
who see the world from their lofty towers,
blinded by wealth,
blinded by power,
will lead us anywhere but further into the dark.

We, who live in the heart of this world,
who feel its pulse in the crowded streets,
the factories, the schools,
must be the ones to raise our voices,
to demand a future we can believe in.

We can no longer pretend.
No more lies, no more hoping the storm will pass.
We stand now,
for truth, for justice,
for the belief that tomorrow can be better,
but only if we fight for it today.

The War for Civility

It is not the color of skin
that holds the whole weight of hatred,
nor the lines of prejudice
that can be traced only to what the eyes can see.
There is something deeper,
buried beneath the surface of our polished words,
our statistics, our politics.
It is in the marrow of our bones,
this tribal, territorial instinct,
once meant for survival in the wild
but now, in civilized life,
a seed of destruction.

We have learned to judge,
to categorize each other not by faces alone,
but by numbers and titles.
The zip code in which you were born
becomes the badge you wear,
the neighborhood, the income bracket,
the number of children in your care,
the degrees hung upon your walls,
these things are weighed, measured,
divided and sorted.
Success or failure,
liberal or conservative,
Republican or Democrat—
we are fractured
into endless slivers of identity.

Do we not see?
This is our modern war,
not of muskets or cannons,
but of silent judgment,
of invisible battle lines drawn
in every statistic, every news headline,
in every whispered conversation
about who belongs
and who does not.

These scripts are ancient,
written into our DNA,
long before the Civil War,

long before the first empire rose
and divided the world into rulers and ruled.
And they are still with us,
in the glances across a crowded room,
in the assumptions we make
about who someone is
based on the smallest of details—
their car, their clothes, their accent,
the way they hold themselves
or the way they hold their pain.

In this war,
we are all soldiers,
armed not with weapons,
but with biases we do not even see.
We march, not in unison,
but in our isolated paths,
following the echo chambers of our own thoughts,
blind to the humanity
that stands on the other side
of our walls of judgment.

And yet, there is hope.
What if, instead of a second civil war,
we fought for civility?
What if we declared a war
not against each other,
but against the darkness in ourselves—
the shadows that whisper,
that pull us into old habits of suspicion,
of fear, of distrust?

This is the war we must fight.
Not to return to the days of old,
to a past that never truly existed,
but to forge a new path,
to transcend the tribalism
that lurks in the corners of our minds.
To rise above the easy labels,
the simple categories
that make it easier to hate,
to turn away,
to justify our indifference.

Civility is not the absence of conflict,
but the presence of compassion
amidst our differences.
It is the act of seeing, truly seeing,
the person across from us,
not as a number,
not as a demographic,
not as a statistic on a government form,
but as a fellow traveler
in this strange and difficult life.

We must wage this war for civility
in every conversation,
in every encounter,
in every choice we make
to listen before speaking,
to question before condemning,
to understand before deciding
who someone is
and what they are worth.

The Civil War of muskets and bayonets
has passed,
but the war for our hearts,
for our collective soul,
rages on.
And we must choose—
do we continue down the path
of division,
of judgment,
of reducing each other
to the sum of our differences?

Or do we rise,
together,
to wage the hardest battle of all—
the battle to reclaim
our shared humanity,
to fight for civility,
not as a luxury,
but as a necessity
for our survival,

for the beauty
of what we could become?

This war,
if we are brave enough to fight it,
will not be won in a single battle.
It will take lifetimes,
generations of unlearning,
of reimagining what it means
to live side by side
in a world of endless complexity.
But the fight is worth it,
for in the end,
it is not about winning or losing,
but about remembering—
remembering that we are all,
in the deepest sense,
one people,
one story,
one hope
for something better

A Pandemic Worse Than COVID

There is a sickness,
worse than any virus,
it spreads in whispers, in shouts,
in the quiet moments when we look away
instead of speaking out.
It fills the air, heavy,
with hatred,
with prejudice,
with the poison of narcissism
that turns every mirror into a weapon.

North and south,
east and west,
no corner untouched,
no heart immune.
It's in the veins of our cities,
the back roads of our towns,
where the flags of extremism wave
and the voices of division drown out the sound
of common ground.

We let it grow,
this pandemic of the mind,
feeding it with our fears,
with the jagged edges of our differences,
until the Commons,
once a space where we all belonged,
cracked,
split apart by walls of ideology,
each brick laid with suspicion
and the cold mortar of indifference.

This is a sickness we created,
allowed to fester and spread,
until every conversation was a battlefield,
every glance a judgment,
every neighbor an enemy.
We destroy what we built
in the name of who is right

and who is wrong,
forgetting that we were once
builders of something greater
than ourselves.

There is no vaccine
for this kind of sickness,
only the fragile hope
that we remember—
the cure lies in us.

Some May Wonder Why I Wrote This Book

Some may wonder why I wrote this book.
Why spill these words onto paper,
why open my heart to the world,
why share the pieces of myself
that are still raw, still healing,
still searching for the light?

Understand this—
I wrote this book
because the world is in need.
Not of more anger,
not of more hatred,
not of more fear.
We've had enough of those
to last us lifetimes.
No, I wrote this book
because we need encouragement—
a quiet reminder
that we are meant to be
something larger,
something beyond
the divisions we carve
into our hearts,
something beyond the darkness
we've let settle into our souls

This world,
our world,
it teeters on the edge
of old wounds
and new battles.
The same ghosts that haunted us
before the Civil War—
they still whisper,
still press their fingers
into the cracks of our unity,
still try to pull us apart.
And if we're not careful,
if we don't see
how fragile we've become,
how quick we are
to turn against each other,

we could find ourselves
on the brink
of a second war,
one with no borders,
no uniforms,
just us—
fighting ourselves,
tearing down what little we've built.

But this book—
this book is my offering,
my way of saying
there is another path.
There is always another path.
These poems,
they are a way to heal,
to stitch together the brokenness
inside myself,
and maybe,
just maybe,
they can help heal
what's broken in you, too.
Because aren't we all
a little broken?
Aren't we all
trying to find a way
to make sense of the world
we've been given,
to leave behind something better
than what we inherited?

I didn't write this book
to point fingers,
to blame or accuse.
I wrote it to remind myself—
and maybe to remind you,
if you're willing to listen—
that life is a gift.
A fragile, fleeting gift,
inhabiting us for a time,
and when it's gone,
it's gone.
So what do we do

with the time we have?
Do we spend it in anger,
in fear,
in bitterness?
Or do we learn
to see the beauty,
the light that still shines
in the darkest places,
the hope that clings
even when everything else falls away.

Some may wonder why I wrote this book.
I wrote it because I believe
we are capable
of more than we've become.
We are capable of kindness,
of compassion,
of love that stretches
beyond the borders of our differences.
We are capable
of leaving the world better
than we found it,
if only we choose to try.

This book,
these words,
they are not an answer.
They are not a solution
to the world's problems.
But they are a beginning.
A beginning of a conversation
about how we move forward,
how we heal,
how we remember
that we are all
in this together.

And maybe,
just maybe,
if we remind each other
that life is a gift,
that we are all fragile,
that we are all capable of beauty,

we can start to build a world
that reflects the best of us,
instead of the worst.

So yes,
I wrote this book.
Not because I have all the answers,
but because I believe in the possibility
of something better.
I believe in the power of words
to heal,
to inspire,
to remind us
of the light that still burns
within each of us,
waiting to be shared.
This is my offering.
This is my hope.
That we remember,
before it's too late,
that we are more than our divisions,
more than our fears,
more than our anger.

We are,
each of us,
a part of something larger,
something more beautiful
than we've allowed ourselves to see.
And that,
in the end,
is why I wrote this book.

Stop!

Stop hiding beneath your red or blue coat,
stop cloaking yourself in colors that divide.
Stop speaking of people in the language of "left" and "right,"
as if humanity could be split by the edges of a page.

Stop pretending you are somebody
because you wear the title Republican or Democrat,
because you feed the media frenzy
that rushes like wildfire into our homes,
igniting every corner with heat, but no light.

Stop putting education above humanity,
as if knowledge alone could absolve you of kindness.
Stop placing religion above humanity,
as if belief makes you pure, while others fall short.

Stop thinking your truths are closer to the center of the world
than those held by others,
stop hating and tearing down because you shake inside,
your life cracked open by unseen fault lines.

Stop believing that just because your candidate won,
you deserve anything more or better—
and if your candidate lost,
you're relieved of your duty to do your part
to make America a better place for everyone.

Stop believing that money and power
entitle you to a larger share of the human spirit,
stop using wealth to buy your way into favor,
into Washington's halls and state capitals,
as if influence could replace integrity.

Stop assuming life is simple,
that it should bend to your will or be cast aside,
stop letting resentment curdle within,
an unchecked fire in your chest.

Stop all these things,
and America will start to heal,
one breath, one word, one choice at a time

Healing as We Move Forward

In the expanse of our nation, divisions carve deep canyons, each conviction a chisel, each belief a blade, sculpting landscapes of discord.

We stand at the crossroads, balancing the scales of security and growth, fairness and opportunity, equality and freedom, each priority a weight, each choice a fulcrum.

Winners bask in the glow of triumph, losers bear the shadows of defeat, yet beneath these labels, we share a common thread, woven into the fabric of a fractured union.

To move forward is to acknowledge the wounds that mar our collective skin, to tend to the scars with empathy, to bridge the chasms with understanding.

Healing is not the absence of pain, but the presence of resolve, a commitment to mend the rifts, to listen beyond the echo chambers, to see beyond the lines drawn in sand.

As we step into the uncertain dawn, let us carry the light of unity, illuminating the path ahead, where differences become dialogue, and diversity becomes strength.

For in the journey of healing, we find the essence of our shared humanity, a testament to resilience, a promise of a future crafted by hands joined in purpose, hearts aligned in hope.

Epilogue

The epilogue of this book captures the Civil War's complex legacy, a battle that closed with a date but left wounds that have never fully healed. It is not just about slavery or the battles fought between the Union and Confederacy; it's about the unresolved tensions that continue to shape America's identity, highlighting the divides among Black and White, North and South, rich and poor. The Civil War was fought to redefine freedom and humanity, but its end in 1865 marked the beginning of a longer struggle—through Reconstruction, Jim Crow, and the civil rights movement—to address the deeply ingrained injustices left behind.

This epilogue speaks to how these historical echoes have rippled into modern times, manifesting in today's polarized America. Now, the fight is no longer just a regional war but one of belief systems—of what America stands for, who gets to belong, and who gets to control its future. The divisions are no longer between North and South but between cities and rural towns, between the left and the right. The rise of misinformation and the resurgence of white supremacy point to a brewing conflict within, with groups like the Proud Boys drawing disturbing parallels to the factionalism of the 19th century. This is not a war of battlegrounds, but of ideologies, where the battlefield is everywhere—from classrooms to social media, to the voting booth.

Out of the rubble of this ideological war, however, rises something profound—Poetry, with its ability to unearth raw truths, begins to shift the energy in America. It brings clarity, exposing the unvarnished truth of a second Civil War, one that may not be fought with guns but with words, policies, and laws that shape who has power and who is left behind. As the political right and left continue to butt heads, poetry finds a way to bypass these rigid lines, bringing light to the deeper wounds that still need healing. In doing so, it evokes a deeper understanding that transcends political labels, speaking to the humanity at the core of every battle. The epilogue warns us that if we are not careful, we may once again tear ourselves apart.

The American Riddle

I am the land of paradox,
the land of promises kept and broken—
Who am I, born from rebellion,
yet wary of change?

I hold within me every shade of belief,
red rivers, blue skies,
the hands of farmers, factory workers, dreamers.
I am the mosaic of conservative and liberal,
a patchwork stitched together by hope,
torn apart by fear—
Can you name me?

I am the past that won't rest,
the future that won't wait,
I am freedom's sharp edge
and the cost of wielding it.
I ask of you: How do we share this vast house,
when each room has its own rules?

I am the anthem sung off-key,
the quiet prayer of the unheard,
the clash of protest and counter-protest,
the storm of voices seeking one truth—
Who can solve me?

I am the soil of prosperity,
but my roots tangle in inequality,
I am the idea of happiness,
dangling just out of reach,
I am the push and pull,
the left hand and the right,
I am the riddle you live inside—
How do we learn to listen?

I am not one or the other,
I am both and beyond.
I am your question, and your answer is yet to come.
What name do you call me?
America—land of the shared,
land of the scarred,
land of the untold possibility.

About the Author

Don Iannone is a highly respected author and expert in economic development and public policy. He is also known by many for his poetry and photography. His new book, The Civil War Yesterday and Today in Poetry, uses poetry to paint a vivid picture of Pre-Civil War America, Civil War America, and Post-Civil War America. It raises the prospect of a new civil war in America, caused by the insurmountable gulf in American's beliefs, values, and expectations for America in the future.

His America's Dream at a Crossroads: The 2024 Presidential Election and Beyond, released in 2024, became a bestseller due to its appeal in view of the 2024 presidential election. Since the book's release on July 8, 2024, Don was interviewed about the book and the upcoming election by over 50 media sources nationwide.

Don led major economic development organizations in Northeast Ohio for eight years and directed the economic and environmental centers at Cleveland State University for fifteen years. From 2000 to 2016, he provided economic development strategy and policy analysis consulting services to over 100 public and private clients in 32 states and internationally. His clients have included several federal agencies and departments, state development agencies, and local and regional economic development and civic organizations. Don has testified before the U.S. Congress and several state legislatures, and he has spoken widely on economic and public policy issues facing communities, regions, and states. He was a faculty member at the University of Oklahoma's Economic Development Institute for 12 years and directed the Ohio Economic Development Education Course for 5 years. Don served on the boards of the American Economic Development Council, National Council for Urban Economic Development, MidAmerica Economic Development Council, and the Ohio Economic Development Association.

Since 2020, he has taught graduate business students at the European Union-based Transcontinental University. Don has authored five nonfiction books and numerous articles and monographs on economic development and public policy. He is also the author of ten earlier poetry collections and ten photographic essays. He holds a doctorate in philosophy and several other degrees. He serves on the board of Seeds of Literacy, a nonprofit dedicated to improving adult literacy in Greater Cleveland. He is active in the International Economic Development Council (IEDC), Cleveland Civil War Roundtable, Literary Cleveland, the Authors Guild, the Academy of American Poets, and the Poetry Society of America. Don and his wife, Mary, a retired Cleveland Clinic executive, live in the Greater Cleveland area.

Glossary

1. 13th, 14th, and 15th Amendments – Constitutional amendments that abolished slavery (13th), granted citizenship and equal protection (14th), and guaranteed voting rights regardless of race (15th).

2. #MeToo – A social movement against sexual harassment and assault, amplifying survivors' voices and advocating for systemic change and accountability.

3. 9/11 – Refers to the September 11, 2001, terrorist attacks in the U.S., leading to significant national and global changes in security, policy, and international relations.

4. "Aspects of the War" Poem – A poem that examines multiple dimensions of the Civil War, including its human, moral, and societal costs.

5. Abolitionists – Activists who sought the immediate end of slavery in the United States before and during the Civil War.

6. Abraham Lincoln – The 16th President of the United States, who led the nation through the Civil War and is known for issuing the Emancipation Proclamation.

7. Adrienne Rich – An influential American poet and essayist known for her work addressing issues of gender, identity, and social justice.

8. Alan Ginsberg – An iconic poet of the Beat Generation, known for works like Howl that critiqued contemporary American culture and politics.

9. Amanda Gorman – A contemporary American poet and activist, best known for her poem The Hill We Climb, which she recited at the 2021 presidential inauguration.

10. American Civil War – A conflict fought between the Northern Union states and the Southern Confederate states from 1861 to 1865, primarily over slavery and states' rights.

11. American Revolution – The war between the American colonies and Great Britain from 1775 to 1783, leading to the founding of the United States.

12. American Sonnets for My Past and Future Assassin – A poetry collection by Terrance Hayes that explores identity, race, and American history through the structure of the sonnet.

13. And Thurlow Weed – A powerful New York journalist and political strategist who played a significant role in shaping the Whig and Republican parties.

14. Andrew Carnegie – A 19th-century industrialist who led the expansion of the U.S. steel industry and became one of the most famous philanthropists of his era.

15. Andrew Johnson – The 17th President of the United States, known for his controversial approach to Reconstruction after the Civil War.

16. Anglo-African – Refers to African Americans of mixed European and African descent, particularly in the context of historical discussions of identity and race.

17. Artificial Intelligence (AI) – The development of computer systems capable of performing tasks that normally require human intelligence, such as speech recognition and decision-making.

18. August Belmont – A financier and diplomat during the Civil War who used his wealth and influence to support the Democratic Party and international diplomacy.

19. Auschwitz – A notorious Nazi concentration and extermination camp during World War II, where millions of Jews and other minorities were murdered.

20. "Battle in the Wilderness" – Refers to the 1864 Civil War battle between Ulysses S. Grant's Union forces and Robert E. Lee's Confederate army, known for its brutal and chaotic combat in dense woods.

21. Battle of Chancellorsville – A major Civil War battle in 1863, where Confederate General Robert E. Lee won a significant but costly victory against Union forces.

22. Battle of Chickamauga – A major 1863 Civil War battle fought in Georgia, resulting in a Confederate victory but high casualties on both sides.

23. Battle of Gettysburg – A pivotal 1863 Civil War battle in Pennsylvania, considered the turning point of the war, resulting in a major Union victory.

24. Battle of Manassas – Also known as the Battle of Bull Run, this was the first major battle of the Civil War, fought in 1861, resulting in a Confederate victory.

25. Battle of New Market – A 1864 Civil War battle in Virginia where Confederate cadets from the Virginia Military Institute famously fought against Union forces.

26. Battle of New Orleans – An 1815 battle during the War of 1812 in which American forces, led by Andrew Jackson, defeated a much larger British force.

27. Battle of Shiloh – A bloody two-day Civil War battle fought in 1862 in Tennessee, marking one of the early large-scale engagements of the war.

28. Battle of Vicksburg – A key 1863 Union victory in the Civil War, which gave the Union control over the Mississippi River and split the Confederacy.

29. Beat Generation – A literary movement of the 1950s, characterized by a rejection of traditional values, exploration of American culture, and a focus on spiritual and sexual liberation.

30. Benjamin Morgan Palmer – A Southern Presbyterian minister known for his sermons defending slavery and supporting the Confederacy.

31. Black Lives Matter – A contemporary social movement advocating for the end of systemic racism and violence against Black individuals.

32. Bob Dylan – An influential American singer-songwriter whose music became anthems for social change during the 1960s and beyond.

33. Brown v. Board of Education – A landmark 1954 Supreme Court case that declared racial segregation in public schools unconstitutional.

34. Buchenwald – A Nazi concentration camp during World War II, where tens of thousands of prisoners, including Jews and political dissidents, were murdered.

35. Camp Chase – A Civil War military camp and prison located in Columbus, Ohio, where Confederate soldiers were held as prisoners of war.

36. Carnifex Ferry – A 1861 battle in West Virginia during the Civil War, leading to a Union victory and further securing control over the region.

37. Chagrin Falls, OH – A small town in Northeast Ohio known for its historic charm and cultural significance, with connections to literature and the arts.

38. Charlottesville, VA 2017 Rally – A white nationalist rally held in Charlottesville, Virginia, which led to violent clashes and the death of a counter-protester.

39. Christian Right – A conservative Christian political movement in the United States that advocates for traditional family values and often opposes LGBTQ+ rights and abortion.

40. Christian Wiman – A contemporary poet and essayist known for his reflections on faith, suffering, and the human experience.

41. Citizen: An American Lyric – A 2014 book by Claudia Rankine that blends poetry, essays, and images to explore race and identity in contemporary America.

42. Civil Rights Movement – A mid-20th-century movement advocating for the legal rights of African Americans, particularly in the areas of voting, education, and desegregation.

43. Claudia Rankine – A Jamaican-American poet and playwright whose work addresses issues of race, identity, and social justice.

44. Clement L. Vallandigham – A leader of the Copperhead faction of anti-war Democrats during the Civil War, known for his opposition to Lincoln's policies.

45. Cleveland Hough Riot – A 1966 race riot in Cleveland's Hough neighborhood, sparked by racial tensions, poverty, and police violence.

46. Cold War – The geopolitical tension and rivalry between the United States and the Soviet Union following World War II, lasting from 1947 to 1991.

47. Colfax Massacre, 1873 – A violent confrontation in Louisiana where white supremacists killed over 100 Black men, symbolizing the failure of Reconstruction efforts.

48. Confederacy – The group of Southern states that seceded from the United States in 1861, sparking the Civil War to preserve their economy, which was heavily dependent on slavery.

49. Conservative Poets – Poets who tend to focus on themes of tradition, order, and a resistance to progressive or revolutionary social change.

50. Contract with America – A 1994 Republican Party legislative agenda that aimed to reduce the size of government and enact conservative reforms.

51. Copperheads – Northern Democrats who opposed the Civil War and sympathized with the Southern cause, advocating for peace with the Confederacy.

52. Cornelius Vanderbilt – A 19th-century American industrialist who built his wealth in railroads and shipping and became one of the richest men in history.

53. Cotton Economy – Refers to the Southern U.S. economy's reliance on the production and export of cotton, which was dependent on slave labor.

54. Cotton Gin – A machine invented by Eli Whitney in 1793 that revolutionized the cotton industry by making it easier to separate cotton fibers from seeds.

55. Cotton Lobby – The group of political and economic interests that supported the cotton industry and defended slavery as essential to its success.

56. "Cotton Boll" Poem – A poem by Sidney Lanier that explores the cultural and economic significance of cotton to the Southern U.S.

57. Cottonwood, 1867 – A poem or literary reference reflecting the post-Civil War era, often touching on themes of reconstruction and the changing South.

58. Covert Racism – Disguised or subtle forms of racism that are embedded in everyday interactions, policies, or societal norms.

59. DACA (Deferred Action for Childhood Arrivals) – A U.S. immigration policy that allows individuals brought to the U.S. as children to receive a renewable two-year period of deferred action from deportation.

60. Dachau – One of the first Nazi concentration camps, established in 1933, and a site of significant atrocities during World War II.

61. Dana Gioia – An American poet and critic who served as the chairman of the National Endowment for the Arts and is known for his advocacy of literary arts.

62. Dave Smith, Poet – A Southern American poet known for his explorations of history, family, and Southern identity in his work.

63. Discrimination – The unjust treatment of different categories of people, particularly on the grounds of race, age, or gender.

64. "Dooryard Bloom'd" Poem – Refers to Walt Whitman's poem When Lilacs Last in the Dooryard Bloom'd, written in response to Abraham Lincoln's assassination.

65. Dred Scott – The African American man at the center of the 1857 Supreme Court case Dred Scott v. Sandford, which ruled that African Americans could not be U.S. citizens.

66. Dylann Roof – A white supremacist who murdered nine African Americans at the Emanuel AME Church in Charleston, South

Carolina, in 2015.

67. Eli Whitney – An American inventor best known for creating the cotton gin, which had a profound impact on the economy and the expansion of slavery in the Southern U.S.

68. Emancipation Proclamation – The 1863 executive order by President Abraham Lincoln that declared the freedom of all enslaved people in Confederate-held territory.

69. Emanuel AME Church – The historic African Methodist Episcopal church in Charleston, South Carolina, where nine people were murdered in a racist attack by Dylann Roof.

70. Emily Dickinson – One of America's greatest poets, known for her innovative, concise style and themes of death, immortality, and nature.

71. Equality – The state of being equal, especially in status, rights, and opportunities.

72. Equity – Fairness and justice in treatment and access, ensuring that people have the support they need to achieve equal outcomes.

73. Fanny M. Jackson – Fanny Jackson Coppin was an African American educator, missionary, and advocate for women's and Black rights during the 19th century.

74. Father Abram Joseph Ryan – A Southern Catholic priest and poet, often referred to as the "Poet-Priest of the Confederacy," known for writing about the Lost Cause.

75. Free Verse Poetry – A style of poetry that does not follow specific rhyme schemes or metrical patterns, allowing for more freedom in expression.

76. Freedman's Bureau – A federal agency established in 1865 to aid freed slaves in the South during the Reconstruction era, providing food, housing, and medical care.

77. Fugitive Slave Act – Laws passed in 1793 and 1850 that required the return of escaped enslaved people to their owners, even if they had fled to free states.

78. George Floyd – An African American man whose murder by a police officer in 2020 sparked widespread protests against police brutality and systemic racism.

79. Gerrymandering – The manipulation of electoral district boundaries to favor one party or class over another.

80. Gilded Age – The period in late 19th-century U.S. history marked by rapid industrialization, economic growth, and social inequality, often masked by a veneer of prosperity.

81. Great Mobile Hurricane, 1865 – A powerful hurricane that struck the Gulf Coast, particularly affecting Mobile, Alabama, in the final year of the Civil War.

82. Great Railroad Strike of 1877 – A nationwide labor strike that began after the Baltimore & Ohio Railroad cut wages for the third time in a year, leading to widespread unrest.

83. Henry Timrod – A Southern poet often called the "Poet Laureate of the Confederacy," who wrote about the Civil War and Southern identity.

84. Henry Ward Beecher – A prominent abolitionist preacher and brother of Harriet Beecher Stowe, known for his fiery sermons against slavery.

85. Herman Melville – An American novelist, short story writer, and poet best known for his novel Moby-Dick and his Civil War poetry collection Battle-Pieces.

86. Iannone, Donald, T. – A contemporary American poet and writer, who is the author of "The Civil War Yesterday and Today in Poetry" and many other poetry and nonfiction books.

87. Immigration – The action of coming to live permanently in a foreign country, often a subject of political debate and policy.

88. Inclusion – The practice or policy of including people who might otherwise be excluded or marginalized, such as those from different races, genders, or abilities.

89. Industrial Revolution – The period of rapid industrial growth during the late 18th and early 19th centuries, marked by the development of machinery and mass production.

90. Industrialization – The process of transforming an economy from agrarian-based to industry-based, typically involving large-scale manufacturing and urbanization.

91. Iron John: A Book About Men – A 1990 book by poet Robert Bly, exploring masculinity through myth, folklore, and psychology.

92. Jack Kerouac – An American novelist and poet, a key figure of the Beat Generation, best known for his novel On the Road.

93. James Baldwin – An American novelist, essayist, and social critic, known for his works on race, sexuality, and identity, including Go Tell It on the Mountain.

94. James Longstreet – A Confederate general during the Civil War, one of Robert E. Lee's most trusted commanders.

95. James Murray Mason – A Confederate diplomat involved in the Trent Affair, sent to Britain to gain support for the Confederate cause.

96. Janis Joplin – A renowned American singer and cultural icon of the 1960s, known for her powerful voice and contributions to rock and blues music.

97. January 6, 2021 Insurrection – A violent attack on the U.S. Capitol by supporters of then-President Donald Trump, attempting to overturn the 2020 presidential election results.

98. Jay Cooke financier – An American financier known for financing the Union war effort during the Civil War by selling government bonds.

99. Jefferson Davis – The President of the Confederate States of America during the Civil War, leading the South in its attempt to secede from the Union.

100. Jerry Falwell – A conservative evangelical pastor and political activist, known for founding the Moral Majority and influencing the

Christian Right movement.

101.Jim Crow Laws – State and local laws enforcing racial segregation in the Southern United States after the Reconstruction period, lasting until the Civil Rights Movement.

102.Jimi Hendrix – An influential American rock guitarist and singer, widely regarded as one of the greatest guitarists in the history of music.

103.Joan Baez – An American folk singer and activist, known for her involvement in the Civil Rights Movement and her music that promoted social change.

104.John Bannon – A Catholic priest and Confederate chaplain who attempted to gain European support for the Confederacy during the Civil War.

105.John Bell (Constitutional Union Party) – A candidate in the 1860 U.S. presidential election, representing the Constitutional Union Party, which sought to avoid secession.

106.John Brown – A radical abolitionist who believed in the violent overthrow of slavery, most famously leading a raid on Harpers Ferry in 1859.

107.John C. Breckinridge (Southern Democratic Party) – The Southern Democratic candidate in the 1860 U.S. presidential election, later a Confederate general and Secretary of War.

108.John D. Rockefeller – An American industrialist and philanthropist, considered the wealthiest American of all time, who founded Standard Oil and became a key figure in the development of the U.S. economy.

109.John Greenleaf Whittier – An American Quaker poet and abolitionist, best known for his anti-slavery writings and his role in the abolitionist movement.

110.John Murray Forbes – A railroad magnate and abolitionist who played a key role in supporting the Union during the Civil War.

111.John Pope – A Union general during the Civil War, best known for his defeat at the Second Battle of Bull Run.

112. John Slidell – A Confederate diplomat involved in the Trent Affair, sent to France to seek support for the Confederacy.

113. Joseph Davis – The brother of Confederate President Jefferson Davis, and a wealthy Mississippi planter who managed one of the largest slave plantations in the South.

114. Joseph McCarthy – A U.S. Senator who became notorious for alleging that large numbers of Communists and Soviet spies had infiltrated the U.S. government during the 1950s, leading to the Red Scare.

115. Joy Harjo – The first Native American Poet Laureate of the United States, known for her works that explore

116. Judah Benjamin – A prominent politician and lawyer in the Confederate government, serving as Attorney General, Secretary of War, and Secretary of State during the Civil War.

117. Kansas-Nebraska Act – An 1854 law that allowed settlers in Kansas and Nebraska territories to decide for themselves whether or not to allow slavery, leading to violent conflict known as "Bleeding Kansas."

118. King Cotton – A term used to describe the economic and political importance of cotton production in the Southern U.S. before the Civil War, emphasizing its influence on the South's economy and international relations.

119. Ku Klux Klan (KKK) – A white supremacist hate group founded in the aftermath of the Civil War, which used terror and violence to oppose Reconstruction and suppress African American rights.

120. Langston Hughes – An influential African American poet and social activist, a key figure in the Harlem Renaissance, known for his work that captures the experience of Black life in America.

121. Layli Long Soldier – A contemporary Native American poet whose work addresses themes of identity, historical trauma, and language, particularly related to indigenous peoples.

122.Leonidas Polk – An Episcopal bishop and Confederate general during the Civil War, known as the "Fighting Bishop."

123.Liberal Poets – Poets who often explore themes of social progress, reform, and inclusivity, frequently advocating for equality and justice in their work.

124.Lines in Long Array Project – A poetry and art project commemorating the 150th anniversary of the Battle of Gettysburg, reflecting on war, memory, and history.

125.Maya Angelou – A celebrated American poet, memoirist, and civil rights activist, known for her powerful works such as I Know Why the Caged Bird Sings and the poem Still I Rise.

126.Memphis Riots, 1866 – A violent racial conflict in Memphis, Tennessee, where white mobs attacked African American communities, exacerbating racial tensions during Reconstruction.

127.Minié Balls – A type of rifle bullet used extensively during the Civil War, known for causing devastating injuries due to its accuracy and range.

128.Missouri Compromise – An 1820 agreement that allowed Missouri to enter the Union as a slave state and Maine as a free state, maintaining the balance of power between free and slave states in Congress.

129.Moncure Daniel Conway – An abolitionist minister who helped lead enslaved people to freedom and became a vocal critic of slavery during the Civil War era.

130.Mulatto – A historical term used to describe a person of mixed white and Black ancestry, often highlighting the racial divides of the time.

131."My Portion is Defeat – today" Poem – A poem reflecting on themes of loss, conflict, and the emotional toll of war or personal defeat.

132.Natasha Trethewey – A former U.S. Poet Laureate whose works often focus on memory, race, and the complexities of Southern history, particularly around Reconstruction.

133.National Anti-Slavery Standard – A prominent abolitionist newspaper founded in 1840 that advocated for the immediate abolition of slavery and equal rights for African Americans.

134.Nazi Party – The far-right political party that ruled Germany from 1933 to 1945 under Adolf Hitler, responsible for the Holocaust and World War II atrocities.

135.Newt Gingrich – A former Speaker of the U.S. House of Representatives and a key figure in the Republican Party's "Contract with America" during the 1990s.

136.Nikki Giovanni – A renowned African American poet and activist, known for her contributions to the Black Arts Movement and her explorations of race, love, and social justice.

137.Northern States list – Refers to the list of states that were part of the Union during the Civil War, opposed to the Southern Confederate states.

138.Ocean Vuong – A contemporary Vietnamese-American poet known for his deeply personal and lyrical explorations of identity, family, and trauma.

139.OVI – Stands for "Ohio Volunteer Infantry," a designation used for military regiments from Ohio that fought for the Union during the Civil War.

140.Pat Robertson – A prominent televangelist and leader of the Christian Right, known for founding the Christian Broadcasting Network and influencing conservative politics.

141.Phillips Brooks – A prominent 19th-century American preacher known for his eloquent sermons and his hymn "O Little Town of Bethlehem," as well as his support for abolition.

142.Pine Ridge Reservation – A Native American reservation in South Dakota, home to the Oglala Lakota, and the site of the 1890 Wounded Knee Massacre.

143.Plantation – Large farms, particularly in the Southern U.S., that relied on enslaved labor to grow cash crops such as cotton and tobacco.

144.Poetry – A literary form that uses heightened language, often with meter, rhyme, and imagery, to express emotions, ideas, and narratives in a concentrated and powerful way.

145. Political Extremism – The holding of extreme political views, often characterized by radical positions that are far outside the accepted norms of political discourse.

146. Political Polarization – The growing divide between political ideologies, often leading to increased partisanship and reduced cooperation across political lines.

147. Prejudice – Preconceived opinions or judgments, often based on stereotypes, that lead to discrimination against individuals or groups.

148. Proud Boys – A far-right extremist group known for its involvement in violent political events, particularly in support of white nationalism and anti-immigrant views.

149. Quakers Meeting of Friends – Refers to a religious meeting of the Religious Society of Friends (Quakers), known for their pacifism and active involvement in social justice movements, including the abolition of slavery.

150. Racism – Discrimination or prejudice based on race, often manifesting as systemic oppression of minority groups by those in power.

151. Ray Kurzweil – A futurist, inventor, and director of engineering at Google, known for his work in artificial intelligence and predictions about the future of humanity and technology.

152. Reconstruction – The period after the Civil War (1865-1877) during which the U.S. government attempted to rebuild and integrate the Southern states into the Union, and to secure rights for newly freed African Americans.

153. Red Scare – A period of intense fear of communism in the United States, particularly after World War I and during the Cold War, leading to widespread suspicion and persecution.

154. Reverend Clementa Pinckney – A state senator and pastor of the Emanuel AME Church in Charleston, South Carolina, who was killed in the 2015 church shooting by Dylann Roof.

155.Reverend Martin Luther King Jr. – A leader of the Civil Rights Movement, known for his advocacy of nonviolent protest and his role in ending legal segregation in the U.S.

156.Rhyme Poetry – A form of poetry that uses repeating patterns of sounds, often at the end of lines, to create rhythm and structure.

157.Rich Mountain – The site of an 1861 Civil War battle in West Virginia, where Union forces secured a strategic victory early in the conflict.

158.Robert Bly – An American poet and leader of the mythopoetic men's movement, known for his work on masculinity and his influential book Iron John.

159.Robert E. Lee – The commanding general of the Confederate Army during the Civil War, known for his leadership in major battles such as Gettysburg and Antietam.

160.Robert Lewis Dabney – A Southern theologian and Confederate chaplain who defended slavery and supported the Confederate cause during the Civil War.

161.Roe v. Wade – The landmark 1973 Supreme Court decision that legalized abortion nationwide, affirming a woman's right to choose.

162.Second Battle of Bull Run – Also known as the Second Battle of Manassas, this 1862 Civil War battle was a decisive Confederate victory in Virginia.

163.Sharecropping – A system of agriculture that developed after the Civil War, in which tenant farmers, often freed slaves, worked a portion of a landowner's land in return for a share of the crops produced.

164.Sidney Lanier – A Southern poet and musician known for his works that reflect the culture and landscape of the post-Civil War South.

165.Slave Market – A public or private venue where enslaved people were bought and sold, a central part of the slave-based economy in the American South.

166.Slavery – The institution in which individuals were owned as property and forced to work without compensation, a key factor leading to the American Civil War.

167.Smithsonian Institution – A group of museums and research institutions in Washington, D.C., founded in 1846 for the increase and diffusion of knowledge.

168.Southern States list – Refers to the list of Southern states that seceded from the Union to form the Confederacy during the Civil War.

169.SS – Short for Schutzstaffel, the paramilitary organization under Adolf Hitler and the Nazi Party, responsible for many of the atrocities committed during the Holocaust.

170.States' Rights – The political doctrine that emphasizes the rights of individual states to govern themselves, a key issue

171.Stephen A. Douglas (Northern Democratic Party) – A U.S. senator from Illinois and the Northern Democratic candidate in the 1860 presidential election, known for his support of popular sovereignty in determining whether states would allow slavery.

172.Steve Scafidi – A contemporary American poet whose work often explores themes of history, politics, and personal experience.

173. Stonewall's bricks: A symbol of resistance representing the 1969 Stonewall Riots, where LGBTQ+ individuals fought back against police oppression at the Stonewall Inn in New York City, sparking the modern gay rights movement.

174.Stonewall Jackson – A Confederate general during the Civil War, known for his tactical brilliance and his role in many key battles, including the First Battle of Bull Run, where he earned his famous nickname.

175.Systemic Racism – The institutional and structural practices that perpetuate inequality and discrimination against racial minorities in various aspects of society, such as education, healthcare, and criminal justice.

176.Tea Party – A conservative political movement in the U.S. that emerged in 2009, advocating for reduced government spending, lower taxes, and limited government regulation.

177. Terrance Hayes – A contemporary American poet known for his innovative use of form and his exploration of race, identity, and culture, particularly in his collection American Sonnets for My Past and Future Assassin.

178. The Rothschilds – A wealthy and influential European banking family, often the subject of conspiracy theories, especially in discussions about international finance and political power.

179. Third Reich – The Nazi regime in Germany from 1933 to 1945, led by Adolf Hitler, responsible for World War II and the atrocities of the Holocaust.

180. Tobacco Economy – The economic system of the Southern U.S. colonies and later states, heavily reliant on the cultivation and export of tobacco, which was often grown using enslaved labor.

181. Tracy K. Smith – An American poet and former U.S. Poet Laureate, known for her explorations of history, identity, and the cosmic and intimate aspects of human experience.

182. Transhumanism – A philosophical movement advocating for the use of advanced technologies to enhance human physical and cognitive abilities, potentially leading to a new phase of human evolution.

183. Treblinka – A Nazi extermination camp in Poland during World War II, where hundreds of thousands of Jews were murdered as part of the Holocaust.

184. Trent Affair – A diplomatic incident during the Civil War in which the U.S. Navy intercepted a British ship, the Trent, and captured two Confederate diplomats, James Mason and John Slidell, nearly causing a war between the U.S. and Britain.

185. Ulysses S. Grant – A Union general during the Civil War who later became the 18th President of the United States; he is known for leading the Union Army to victory and his efforts to protect African American rights during Reconstruction.

186. Underground Railroad – A secret network of routes and safe houses

used by enslaved African Americans to escape to free states and Canada, often aided by abolitionists.

187. Union – Refers to the Northern states that remained loyal to the U.S. government during the Civil War and fought to preserve the nation and abolish slavery.

188. Urbanization – The process by which rural areas become more urban, often associated with industrialization and the migration of people to cities for work and economic opportunities.

189. Wade in the Water – A spiritual associated with the Underground Railroad, its lyrics symbolizing both baptism and escape from slavery through water routes.

190. Walt Whitman – An American poet, essayist, and journalist, considered one of the most influential poets in American literature, best known for his collection Leaves of Grass and his Civil War-era poetry.

191. Watts Riot – A major race riot in the Watts neighborhood of Los Angeles in 1965, sparked by issues of police brutality and economic inequality, which resulted in widespread violence and destruction.

192. Whereas (poetry book) – A collection of poems by Layli Long Soldier that addresses the language of treaties and the history of Native American displacement and resistance.

193. White Supremacy – The belief in the superiority of white people over people of other racial backgrounds, often manifesting in discriminatory policies, systemic racism, and acts of violence.

194. Wilkinson County, MS – A county in Mississippi known for its historical connection to the cotton economy and plantation slavery, as well as being the home of the Davis Bend Plantation owned by Joseph Davis, the brother of Jefferson Davis.

195. William Haines Lytle – A Union general and poet who was killed during the Battle of Chickamauga; he was also known for his poem "Antony and Cleopatra."

196. William Slade – An African American abolitionist and educator, who played a key role in the anti-slavery movement and worked to

improve education for African Americans.

197. Woodstock – A 1969 music festival that became a symbol of the counterculture movement, known for its advocacy of peace, love, and music, attracting iconic performers and a large audience.

198. Wounded Knee – The site of two historical events: an 1890 massacre of Lakota Sioux by U.S. troops and a 1973 standoff between Native American activists and federal authorities, both marking significant moments in Native American history.

199. Yusef Komunyakaa – An African American poet known for his work addressing themes of war, memory, and race, including his Pulitzer Prize-winning collection Neon Vernacular.

200. Zora Neale Hurston – An influential writer and anthropologist, a key figure in the Harlem Renaissance, best known for her novel Their Eyes Were Watching God.

201. Zouaves – A light infantry regiment known for their distinctive, colorful uniforms, originally formed in French North Africa, with some regiments serving in both the Union and Confederate armies during the Civil War.

239

240